Skills for Employability

StepUP

B2

Coursebook and eBook

CB131218

Lynn Bonesteel
Carmella Lieske
Robyn Brinks Lockwood
Nancy Blodgett Matsunaga
Bridget McLaughlin
Azra Uslu

Step Up B2

Pearson Education, 221 River Street, Hoboken, NJ 07030 USA

Cover Illustration: Roy Hermelin

Text composition: Straive

Library of Congress Cataloging-in-Publication Data: A catalog record for the print edition is available from the Library of Congress.

Printed in the United States of America

ISBN-13: 978-0-13-747363-2

1 2023

Acknowledgments

We would like to thank the following people for their help with this project.

Güzide Göksen Birol, Istanbul Okan University; **Eduardo Pinell Campuzano,** CIU Director, Universidad Privada Franz Tamayo; **Meg Cassamally,** University of Siena; **Adrian Crawley,** Evority Learning Centre; University of Siena; **Yabancı Diller,** School of Foreign Languages; **Louise Dixon,** Director of Studies at Hallo! Servizi Linguistici; **Aybala Eren,** Gazi University; **Alex Fayle,** Well & Will Language Academy; **Elizabeth Cruz Flores,** Tecnológico de Monterrey; **Jacques Friggieri,** Redrob; **María Amparo Garcia,** ICPNA Cusco; **Christina Gebbia,** Director of Let's Talk English Center in Valencia; **Maria de la Paz Giglio,** New Concept School of English; **Zeynep Güler,** İstanbul Okan University; **Ilaria Incorvaia,** ITIS 'Antonio Meucci', Florence; **Nancy Johnstone,** School of Engineering, UBA, Buenos Aires, Argentina; **Sevil Altıkulaçoğlu Kayaer,** Gazi University; **Yeliz Korkmaz,** Yıldız Technical University, Turkey; **Héctor Raúl Sánchez Lozano,** Proulex Universidad de Guadalajara; **Mariana Juana Aviles Martillo,** coordinator of CEFI, Center for Continuing Educatiòn and Interamerican Labor; **Anne Marie Mc Gowan,** University of Rome 'Tor Vergata' Italy; **Cristian Meléndez,** Universidad Católica de El Salvador; **Jose Manuel Mendivil S.,** Centro Boliviano Americano - Fundación Cultural y Educativa La Paz; **Paul Cruz Montenegro,** English Coordinator of CRC - Peru Cruceros; **M.Àngels Nogué,** Centre D'Idiomes Olot; **Irem Ozcan,** Gazi University, College of Foreign Languages; **Claudia Posarelli,** ITIS Meucci Firenze; **Steven Pragnell,** Astex Servicios Lingüísticos, Madrid; **María de Lourdes Camarillo Rodríguez,** Escuela Bancaria y Comercial; **Raquel Sánchez,** Faculty of Education in Albacete (UCLM); **Chayapak Tangapiwut,** Burapha University Language Institute; **Onur Uludag,** Yildiz Technical University; **Taku Umeda,** Tokyo Business and Language College; **Laura Vacca,** Inglese su Misura; **Marijke van Leuven,** Oxford School of English, Verona, Italy.

Photo Credits Page 2 (1): Shutterstock; 2 (2): Shutterstock; 2 (3): GLimages/Shutterstock; 2 (4): Undrey/Shutterstock; 2 (5): Barock/Shutterstock; 2 (6): Air Images/Shutterstock; 5: Mark Bowden/123RF; 6 (top): Shutterstock; 6 (bottom): MintImages/Shutterstock; 9: Ground Picture/Shutterstock; 11 (1): Mila Supinskaya Glashchenko/Shutterstock; 11 (2): Dragon Images/Shutterstock; 11 (3): Fizkes/Shutterstock; 11 (4): Shutterstock; 12 (top left): Cast Of Thousands/Shutterstock; 12 (top center): Cast Of Thousands/Shutterstock; 12 (top right): Rachata Teyparsit/Shutterstock; 12 (bottom left): Dean Drobot/Shutterstock; 12 (bottom center): Cookie Studio/Shutterstock; 12 (bottom right): Ground Picture/Shutterstock; 13: Daniel Jenny/Shutterstock; 14 (left): Daniel M Ernst/Shutterstock; 14 (right): Black Kings/Shutterstock; 16 (Mehmet Ali): GaudiLab/Shutterstock; 16 (Emily Moore): Kinga/Shutterstock; 16 (Richard Thompson): Fizkes/Shutterstock; 16 (Ju Yang): Amnaj Khetsamtip/Shutterstock; 17: Kateryna Onyshchuk/Shutterstock; 18 (email icons): WonderfulPixel/Shutterstock; 19: Fizkes/Shutterstock; 21: Vadym Pastukh/Shutterstock; 23 (pizza): FARBAI/Shutterstock; 23 (microphone): Sammby/Shutterstock; 23 (plastic tube): EgudinKa/Shutterstock; 23 (leaf on plastic tube): Mallinka1/Shutterstock; 24: Dilok Klaisataporn/Shutterstock; 25: KeyStock/Shutterstock; 27: BearFotos/Shutterstock; 27 (social media icons): Rashad Ashur/Shutterstock; 27 (web media icons): VectorForever/Shutterstock; 29: Photonimo/Shutterstock; 30 (left): Vladimir Mulder/Shutterstock; 30 (right): SaitoFAM/Shutterstock; 31 (left): DedMityay/Shutterstock; 31 (right): ViDI Studio/Shutterstock; 32 (Wang): Kathy Hutchins/Shutterstock; 32 (Einstein): PictureLux/The Hollywood Archive/Alamy Stock Photo; 32 (Hamilton): Brian A. Witkin/Shutterstock; 33 (top left): Fizkes/Shutterstock; 33 (top right): Mallika Home Studio/Shutterstock; 33 (bottom left): Jacek Chabraszewski/Shutterstock; 33 (bottom right): Dean Drobot/Shutterstock; 34: Tonktiti/Shutterstock; 36 (top left): Gorodenkoff/Shutterstock; 36 (top right): Photographielove/Shutterstock; 36 (bottom left): Sunshine Seeds/Shutterstock; 36 (bottom right): Iryna Inshyna/Shutterstock; 37 (left): ESB Professional/Shutterstock; 37 (right): Wjarek/Shutterstock; 38 (Jacek): Wavebreakmedia/Shutterstock; 38 (Ariane): Diego Cervo/Shutterstock; 38 (Dwayne): Minerva Studio/Shutterstock; 40 (food donation): Irina Strelnikova; 40 (volunteers): N.Savranska/Shutterstock; 40 (help animals) Macrovector/Shutterstock; 40 (helping seniors): Mascha Tace/Shutterstock; 41: Vectorfusionart/Shutterstock; 42 (Andre Williams top): VK Studio/Shutterstock; 42 (SurferBoy98 avatar): VK Studio/Shutterstock; 42 (surfer): Yuval Beraru/Shutterstock; 42 (SurferBoy98 avatar): VK Studio/Shutterstock; 42 (Bill Baxter avatar): Iofoto/Shutterstock; 42 (SurferBoy98 avatar): VK Studio/Shutterstock; 44: Net Vector/Shutterstock; 45: Airdone/Shutterstock; 46 (Carrie, top): Ground Picture/Shutterstock; 46 (Paul, left): AJR_photo/Shutterstock; 46 (Himari, center): Natu/Shutterstock; 46 (Elena, right): El Nariz/Shutterstock; 47 (Paul, top): AJR_photo/Shutterstock; 46 (Himari, center): Natu/Shutterstock; 046 (Elena, bottom): El Nariz/Shutterstock; 48: LanKogal/Shutterstock; 49: ESB Professional/Shutterstock; 50 (top): Ferli/123RF; 50 (bottom): Pormezz/Shutterstock; 51: Racorn/123RF; 52: Fizkes/Shutterstock; 75 (woman and man avatars): Gurza/Shutterstock; 77 (woman and man avatars): Gurza/Shutterstock; 79 (woman and man avatars): Gurza/Shutterstock; 81 (woman and man avatars): Gurza/Shutterstock; 83 (woman and man avatars): Gurza/Shutterstock; 85 (woman and man avatars): Gurza/Shutterstock.

Scope and Sequence

Welcome	
pages 2–4	In the classroom | Learn about your book | Meet your Employability Skills Coaches

Module	I can . . .	Learning Objectives	Vocabulary
1 **Communication 1** Active Listening pages 5–8	I can explain the importance of and describe specific strategies for active listening.	• Recognize the three parts of active listening • Explain the importance of active listening • Describe specific strategies that show active listening	*attentive, clarify, engage, expand, focus, impatient, multitask, non-verbal cue, refresh, retain*
2 **Communication 2** Building Rapport pages 9–12	I can explain work rapport and describe strategies for building and maintaining it.	• Explain what rapport is and its role in good work relationships • Describe specific strategies for building rapport • Describe specific strategies to maintain rapport	*at ease, atmosphere, common ground, establish, foundation, harmonious, inappropriate, interact, mutual, open, shut someone down*
3 **Goal Setting** Strategic Career Goals pages 13–16	I can explain the importance of strategic career goals and identify skills and steps to reach them.	• Explain the importance of strategic career goals • Describe how to use short-term goals as stepping stones • Explain when and how goals should be re-aligned • Describe specific strategies to transfer skills to a new career	*adjust, long-term, pursue, re-align, short-term, start from scratch, stepping stone, timeline, transferable skills*
4 **Teamwork** Preventing and Managing Group Conflict pages 17–20	I can explain causes of group conflict and describe strategies for preventing and managing conflict.	• Explain the common causes of conflict • Describe specific strategies to prevent conflict • Describe specific strategies to manage conflict	*acknowledge, brainstorm, compromise, critical, defensive, diversity, escalate, foster, inclusive, morale, prevention*
5 **Critical Thinking** Evaluating Information pages 21–24	I can describe specific strategies for evaluating information.	• Describe specific strategies to evaluate the credibility of a claim • Describe specific strategies to evaluate the reliability of the evidence • Explain three strategies to evaluate the logic of the evidence	*bias, cite, claim, credible, evidence, flaw, logical, reliable, statistics, vague, verify*
6 **Leadership** Building Leadership Skills pages 25–28	I can describe important skills of good leaders and strategies for good leadership.	• Describe five specific skills that good leaders use • Explain how to develop these skills	*challenge, collaboration, constructive, delegate, effective, empower, micromanage, motivate, persuasion, pushback, resistant, vision*

Pronunciation	Language Strategy	Project	Talk!
Pronouncing *th*	Clarify and paraphrase	Use an active listening strategy in a real-life situation	Discuss facts about active listening
The letter *s*	Listen for tone	Interview people who have good rapport skills	Use icebreakers to develop rapport
Weak pronunciation of *has* and *have*	Listen for context clues to understand idioms	Interview a person who followed a plan to achieve their goal	Figure out long-term goals and strategies to reach them
Syllables and stress with adjective endings	Listen for purpose or cause and effect	Interview people about their conflict management strategies	Compare different types of communication at work in terms of preventing and managing conflict
Consonant groups	Identify referents for the pronouns *one*, *this*, and *it*	Evaluate the credibility of a chosen source of information	Discuss challenges around finding trustworthy sources for information or news
Contractions with *will*	Listen to make predictions	Research a leader you admire and describe their leadership skills	Choose your own board of directors

Module	I can . . .	Learning Objectives	Vocabulary
7 **Self-Management** Persistence pages 29–32	I can describe the importance of persistence and specific strategies to develop the *yet* attitude.	• Explain what persistence is and why it is important • Explain what the *power of yet* is and how it can affect your mindset • Describe specific strategies to develop persistence and the *yet* attitude	*capacity, discouraged, encounter, input, obstacle, optimism, overcome, overwhelming, potential, renewed, setback, stumble*
8 **Wellness** Improving Your Wellness pages 33–36	I can explain the habits and importance of wellness and describe specific strategies for improving it.	• Explain the importance of evaluating personal routines to improve wellness • Describe ways to replace unhealthy habits with healthy ones • Describe ways to maintain healthy habits	*athletic, diet, drain, encompass, habit, meditate, nutritious, priority, proven, replace*
9 **Social Responsibility** Giving Back pages 37–40	I can explain the benefits of social responsibility and describe ways to give back.	• Explain the benefits of giving back to the community for individuals and businesses • Describe ways companies give back to the community or society • Describe ways employees can give back when their company doesn't have programs • Describe ways to give back when you aren't working for a company	*capable, cause, donation, drive, fundraiser, incentive, moral, network, obligation, participate, reputation, volunteer*
10 **Branding** Branding Yourself Online pages 41–44	I can describe strategies for developing my personal online brand.	• Describe essential things to consider when building your brand online • Explain how to network online and use social media to advance my career • Describe specific strategies for protecting my information • Explain how to tell my story	*consistent, genuine, perception, portray, presence, privacy settings, relevant, selective, temperament, visible, work ethic*
11 **Job Search** Researching Companies pages 45–48	I can describe the benefits of and specific strategies for researching companies during the job-search process.	• Describe specific strategies to research companies • Explain where and how to find specific, in-depth company information • Explain the benefits of researching companies	*at a glance, background work, business plan, due diligence, inside scoop, keyword search, knowledge base, long-term prospects, mission statement, narrow the field, perfect fit, work-life balance*
12 **Interviewing** Difficult Interview Questions pages 49–52	I can describe strategies for answering both common and difficult interview questions.	• Describe specific strategies to answer common interview questions • Explain how best to prepare for an interview • Describe techniques to deal with challenging interview questions	*buy time, emphasize, on the spot, present, self-doubt, strategy, stump, take the lead*

Pronunciation	Language Strategy	Project	Talk!
The *-ed* endings in adjectives	Listen for explanations	Interview someone with a positive attitude to learn about their strategies and solutions when facing problems	Learn about four famous people who persisted and then reached their goals
The letter *a*	Listen for main ideas and details	Research ways to improve your wellness and write five healthy habits that you want to try	Discuss wellness practices around the world
Linking identical consonants	Listen for transition words of addition	Research or interview someone about programs at work for giving back	Ways to volunteer if you do not have much time
Linking a vowel to a vowel	Read to identify supporting reasons	Interview two people with a strong, successful online presence	Discuss social media facts about job seekers and employers
Stressed syllables in nouns	Collocations	Research a company you would like to know more about	Discuss your priorities when job hunting
Weak and blended pronunciation of *to*	Euphemisms	Search for difficult interview questions and then answer them	Discuss statistics on interview behavior

To the Teacher

Overview

Step Up is a flexible online course designed for adults or young adults who want to improve their employability skills—whether to get a first job, secure a promotion, find a different job, re-enter the workforce after an absence, or change fields. Although the emphasis of the course is on employability skills, *Step Up* also develops English language skills by providing vocabulary instruction and practice, listening, reading, and notetaking skills, pronunciation practice, and discussion strategies.

Levels

There are six levels of *Step Up*, CEFR A2+ to C1, Global Scale of English (GSE) 34 to 84.

***Step Up* level**	**GSE**
Step Up A2+	34–43
Step Up B1	41–51
Step Up B1+	49–58
Step Up B2	56–66
Step Up B2+	64–75
Step Up C1	73–84

Two Versions of *Step Up*

Students can study the *Step Up* course in two ways: as a self-study course or as a self-study plus course, which is the self-study course combined with a teacher-led class. As a self-study course, each level of *Step Up* takes students 18 hours to complete, though this may vary as it is self-paced. The teacher-led course provides 14 hours of class time, with additional resources and extension activities available in the Teaching Notes, which would extend class time.

Student's Components

	Self-study course	**Self-study plus course**
Online Course	✓	✓
Coursebook + eBook or eBook only	✗	✓
Resources (online)	✓	✓

Teacher's Components

	Self-study plus course
Coursebook and/or eBook	✓
Access to the Online Course	✓
Teaching Notes	✓
Resources (online)	✓

The Online Course

Students study the following 12 modules, of which the first nine are **personal and social capabilities** and the last three are job-seeking skills:

Module 1 Communication 1	**Module 2** Communication 2	**Module 3** Goal Setting
Module 4 Teamwork	**Module 5** Critical Thinking	**Module 6** Leadership
Module 7 Self-Management	**Module 8** Wellness	**Module 9** Social Responsibility
Module 10 Branding	**Module 11** Job Search	**Module 12** Interviewing

Each module has an employability skills coach—an animated character—who takes the students through the 10 steps of the module. Step 11 is a progress check; it includes a practice test and a graded test. If the student scores at least 70% on every graded test, they are given access to the final exam. If they score at least 80% on this assessment, they receive a certificate of completion.

For a closer look at the online course, please see the Online Module Walkthrough in the Teacher Resources.

Coursebook/eBook

The Coursebook/eBook is made up of two main sections: the modules and the back matter.

The Modules

Welcome module

The Coursebook begins with a Welcome module, which is comprised of four sections to:

- help students get to know each other and form a community of learners
- provide students with useful language they need to work effectively in class
- help students navigate the Coursebook so they get the most out of it
- introduce students to the 12 employability skills coaches they meet in the online course.

The 12 Employability Skills Modules

Following the Welcome Module are the 12 employability skills modules, corresponding to each module in the online course. Students need to do each online module before they come to class. In class, you guide them through each module to reinforce what they have learned online, to deepen their understanding of the material, and to share how they can apply what they have learned to their own lives.

Back Matter

There are four sections in the back of the Coursebook and eBook:

- *Check your understanding* enables students to demonstrate they have understood the material they have studied online and gives them an opportunity to clear up any misunderstandings at the beginning of a class.
- *Discussion strategies* provide students with four different sets of strategies that can help them engage in class. These include how to work with others; clarify what you hear or clarify what you say; get and stay involved in the discussion; and organize your ideas. Audio models enable students to practice their pronunciation.
- *Vocabulary practice* gives students additional practice with the vocabulary they have learned in the online course. The first activity is a word puzzle, and the second activity uses the target words from the puzzle in context. The answers are provided in the eBook and in the Resources folder.
- *The Glossary* provides the definitions of some words or phrases printed in light brown in the Coursebook to facilitate understanding.

Flexibility

While the sequence of the modules is fixed in the coursebook, you can change the sequence to meet the needs of your students. You may want to have the class review the scope and sequence and vote on which modules to do first. If you change the sequence, we suggest you create a syllabus and upload it to the platform.

Resources for Students

All audio and video files for the online course and all audio files for the coursebook are accessible within the activities in the course. In addition, these audio and video files are also available in the Resources, to allow students to watch or listen whenever they wish without going to the lesson itself. Also included in the Resources are the reading texts, as well as answer keys to the *Vocabulary practice* in the Coursebook.

Resources for Teachers

Teaching Notes

There are general teaching notes to help you get the most out of the course. Then there are notes for each module that begin with an overview of the online module that synopsizes what the students have learned online. Following the overview are teaching notes for each step in the coursebook, including tips, extensions, culture notes, and more.

Module Walkthrough

There is also a module walkthrough that visually describes a module and the underlying pedagogy for both the online course and the coursebook.

Platform Support

To help you navigate the platform and use all the tools available, there is a guided tour when you first log on to Pearson English Connect. In addition, you will find numerous resources under the "Help" button to orient you to the platform. And to get in touch with support, you can click on Help>Documentation>Contact Support.

Welcome

① In the classroom

A Get to know your classmates

Talk to your classmates. Find someone who matches each prompt. Write their first name.

Find someone who...

- has received good news this month ____________
- had a hard time getting to class ____________
- can recommend a funny TV show ____________
- knows how they would spend $1 million ____________
- broke a bone when they were a child ____________
- solved a technology problem this week ____________

B Useful language

Complete the conversations with sentences from the box. Then listen and check your answers.

a	~~Can you repeat the instructions?~~	**d**	What's the English word for "barato"?
b	How do you pronounce this word?	**e**	you're saying we should do this for homework?
c	What's the difference between "advice" and "advise"?	**f**	Could you explain that a bit more?

1

2

3

4

5

6

C Role play

PAIRS **Choose a conversation from 1B and role play it. Use different information.**

② Learn about your book

1 How many modules are in the course?

a 5 **b** 9 **c** 11 **d** 12

2 How many steps are in each module?

a 6 **b** 7 **c** 8 **d** 9

3 Look at this icon on page 5.
It tells you to go to page 68.
Read what is on that page.
How can you use that information?

DISCUSSION STRATEGIES
Go to page 68.

____

4 On page 5, Exercise C says Check your understanding. Go to page 54. What is on that page?

a questions to test vocabulary
b questions to ask my teacher
c questions to review the Online Course
d questions to ask my partner

5 Look through Module 1. Which Steps in the book refer to Steps in the Online Course?

a Steps 1, 2, and 3
b Steps 2, 5, and 7
c Steps 3, 4, and 6
d Steps 5, 6, and 7

6 Look at the I-can statement after Step 7 in each module, for example

I can identify successful communication skills. ☐

What is it for?

____

7 What will you find on pages 72–83?

a listening practice
b grammar practice
c vocabulary practice
d pronunciation practice

8 What will you find on pages 86–87?

a a glossary
b listening activities
c vocabulary practice
d an audio script

To find the answers for CHECK YOUR UNDERSTANDING and VOCABULARY PRACTICE you can look in your ebook or use the answer key in the Student's Resources online.

Meet your Employability Skills Coaches

MODULE 1
Greetings! I'm Dr. Jabu Cele. I have my doctorate in communications and I'm a senior vice president at one of the world's top marketing companies.

MODULE 2
Hi there! I'm Emma Lu, and I'll be your coach for the Communication 2 module. I'm a corporate teamwork coach.

MODULE 3
Hello there. I'm Zehra Teke and I'll be your Employability Skills coach for the module about Goal Setting. I'm a business consultant with a master's degree in management.

MODULE 4
Hello! My name is Kristine Ross. I'm the human resources manager for a large, international company. I'll be your coach for the Teamwork module.

MODULE 5
Hello. My name is Marek Kamiński. I'm an investigative journalist and I'll be your Employability Skills coach for the Critical Thinking module.

MODULE 6
Hi, I'm Sonia Lopez. I'll be your coach for the Leadership module. I'm the Chief Executive Officer—the CEO—of the Alacarte Restaurant Group.

MODULE 7
Hello, my name is Felix Becker. I'm a professional certified life coach and I'll be your coach for the Self-Management module.

MODULE 8
Hello and welcome to the Wellness module. I'll be your Employability Skills coach. My name is Kai Sugimoto. I have a PhD in psychology and I do research on health and wellness.

MODULE 9
Hello, there. My name is Ana Silva. I'm the coordinator of social responsibilty for a large company and I am your coach for the Social Responsibilty module.

MODULE 10
Hi. Welcome to the Branding module. I'm Rakesh Patel, and I'm your Employability Skills coach. I work in marketing.

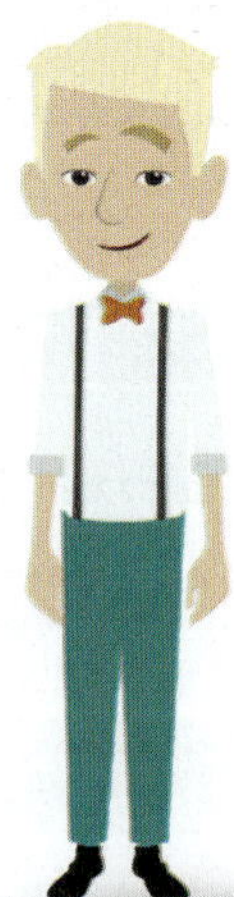

MODULE 11
Hello! Welcome. I'm Justin Roy, and I'm your coach for the Job Search module. I'm a career advice blogger and my goal is to help people find their dream jobs.

MODULE 12
Hi. My name is Aisha Omar. I'm a career counselor at the U.S. Department of Labor and I'll be your coach for the Interviewing module.

1
MODULE

Communication 1

Active Listening

DISCUSSION STRATEGIES

Go to page 68.

Step 1 Get started

A Refresh your memory! Watch the *What You'll Learn* video.

B Look at the photo. Are all the people using good active listening strategies? Why or why not?

C Check your understanding. Go to page 54.

Step 2 Tell your story

A THINK In your online course, you thought about a time you needed active listening skills at work, school, or in your personal life. What happened and what did you learn? Listen to the example.

B PAIRS Discuss your story.

C SHARE Tell your story to the class.

Step 3 Activate your knowledge

A PAIRS Listen to a conversation between Sarah and Pietro, who are web designers on a project together. Pietro has just met with their clients and is filling Sarah in on the details. Pay attention to how each person uses active listening skills. What are they doing correctly or incorrectly? Check the boxes and discuss if you think this was a successful conversation or not.

This person ...	Pietro	Sarah
1 is taking notes	☐	☐
2 is paraphrasing sentences	☐	☐
3 is asking questions for clarification	☐	☐
4 seems distracted	☐	☐
5 is multi-tasking	☐	☐
6 sometimes interrupts	☐	☐
7 sounds impatient	☐	☐
8 sometimes finishes the other person's sentences	☐	☐

B PAIRS Choose if you are Student A or B. Study your card and perform the role play with your partner using your own ideas and the active listening strategies from the online module. Then give each other feedback on how well you felt the other person was listening.

Student A

You are an employee at a small gift and souvenir shop. Your boss is going to talk to you about changing the store display.

- *You are counting the cash in the cash drawer when your boss starts talking to you. Ask your boss to wait a minute so you can write down the number and then start taking notes.*
- *Make sure you understand exactly what changes your boss is describing. Paraphrase and ask questions for clarification.*
- *Ask if you need to change around everything in the entire store.*
- *As you are listening, there are customers already coming in. It's a busy weekend day and you are not sure this is the best day to make the changes.*

Student B

You are the owner of a small gift and souvenir shop. You need to talk to an employee about changing the store display.

- *The ceramic vases are very popular and should be placed in the window to attract more customers.*
- *The USB drives should be closer to the cash register. They are small and easy to steal, so they need to be where you can see them.*
- *In general, you want to give the store a "cleaner" look, for example, by adding more space between items.*
- *You have a lot of errands to run and won't be in the store. You need your employee to take care of this today.*
- *You are in a rush so you are a little impatient as you describe the changes to your employee.*

Step 4 Take away

A Complete the table with the **Dos** and **Don'ts** and their reasons from the list.

- Ask questions
- Refresh memory
- Check you've understood
- Make eye contact

- Finish someone's sentences
- Keep phone or laptop open
- You will have a turn to speak
- It's disrespectful

Dos	Reason
Take notes	
	Shows you're listening
Paraphrase	
	Clarify information

Don'ts	Reason
	Can distract you
Multi-task	
	Not polite and you can't be sure what the other is going to say
Show signs of feeling impatient	

B PAIRS Compare your charts. Discuss which of the Dos you find easy or difficult to use when listening and any Don'ts that you sometimes do without thinking.

Step 5 Project

PAIRS In your online course, you chose an active listening strategy from this module and then used it in a situation where you needed to actively listen. Explain what the situation was and how well the strategy worked. Read the example.

I tried taking notes during a meeting with my manager. We're usually really busy and there isn't time. But this time I asked her to wait a minute so I could take notes. She actually seemed to appreciate it; she could see I was trying to pay attention. It was really helpful in the end because I got all the details I needed without having to go back and ask questions.

Step 6 Talk!

PAIRS Listening is something that we just do without thinking. However, we have all been in situations where we suddenly realize that we haven't been listening to a word of what the other person has been saying! Read these facts about listening.

75% of the time, we are distracted, preoccupied, or forgetful.

After listening to someone talk, we can *immediately* recall about **50%** of what was said, but it's even less if we didn't like the subject or the person!

We **listen** at **125–150** words per minute, but **think** at **1,000–3,000** words per minute.

85% of what we have learned is through listening (not talking or reading).

One hour later, we remember less than **20%** of what we heard.

Less than **2%** of the population has had formal education on how to listen.

- Do any of the facts surprise you? Why?
- Do you they remind you of interactions that you have had?
- Are there any facts that help you understand some of the things you do?

Step 7 Going forward

A PAIRS In your online course, you reflected on what situations in your life you will handle differently after studying more about active listening. Discuss. Listen to the examples.

B SHARE Present your ideas to the class.

VOCABULARY PRACTICE
Go to page 74.

I can explain the importance of and describe specific strategies for active listening. ☐

2

MODULE

Communication 2

Building Rapport

DISCUSSION STRATEGIES

Go to page 68.

Step 1 Get started

A Refresh your memory! Watch the *What You'll Learn* video.

B Look at the photo. Do the people have good rapport with each other? How do you know? Why is it important to build rapport with people at work?

C Check your understanding. Go to page 55.

Step ② Tell your story

A THINK In your online course you thought about a time you built rapport at work, school, or in your personal life. What did you do and what was the effect? Listen to the example.

B PAIRS Discuss your story.

C SHARE Tell your story to the class.

Step ③ Take away

A GROUPS of 3–5 Review your notes from the online module and complete the chart. Fill in examples of at least five strategies you can use to build and maintain rapport.

Building and maintaining rapport	Strategies
With body language	*greet people with a smile*
With conversation	
With your attitude and actions	

B SHARE Check your answers with the class.

Step 4 Activate your knowledge

A PAIRS **Brainstorm. What are some specific ways you can build rapport in the following situations? Work together to think of at least three questions, conversation starters, or conversation topics that you could use for each situation.**

1 A new person has just been hired at the company where you work. You meet him in the breakroom.

a. Hello, I'm Petra

b. ____________________

c. ____________________

2 You're at a meeting at your workplace. You meet someone you've never met before who works in another part of the business.

a. ____________________

b. ____________________

c. ____________________

3 You work in the same office on different teams. You sometimes check in with each other.

a. ____________________

b. ____________________

c. ____________________

4 You work in a store and need to help the customers.

a. ____________________

b. ____________________

c. ____________________

B PAIRS **Which of the scenarios would you find the most challenging? Why? What can you do to make it less so? Discuss.**

Step 5 Project

PAIRS In your online course, you interviewed 2–3 people you know who have good rapport skills and asked them how they build and maintain rapport. Share the information you learned with your partner. Read the example.

My co-worker told me she learned how to build rapport when she worked at a restaurant. Every day she met total strangers and had to treat them like friends. So, she would smile a lot and use body language and gestures to show warmth. And she would try to have real conversations with her customers. Now, this person is one of the friendliest people in my office. She checks in with people every day, even if it's just to say, "How are you?" or "How was your weekend?" I asked her if she thinks this helps her build relationships at work and she said, "Yes, definitely."

Step 6 Talk!

PAIRS One way to build rapport is to use interesting questions to encourage conversation and discover what you have in common. **Icebreakers** are conversation topics or activities that people use to get to know each other in a fun, relaxing way. Discuss the icebreakers below. Use the questions to guide your conversation.

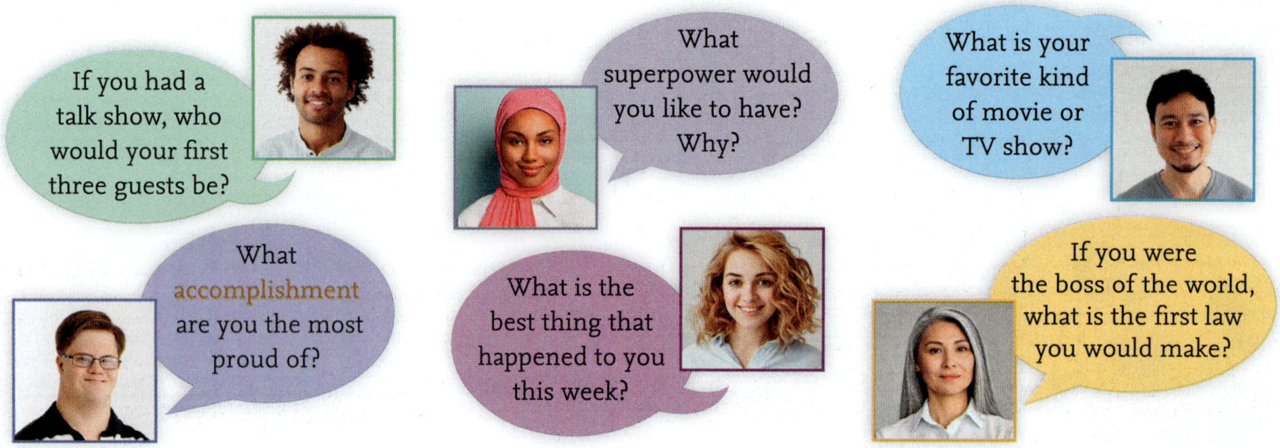

- Would you use any of the above questions to start a conversation? Why or why not?
- What other questions do you think would be good icebreakers?
- What are the best topics to start a conversation? Are there any topics that are good to avoid?
- Have you ever played an icebreaker activity as part of a team-building session? What was it? Did you enjoy it?

Step 7 Going forward

A PAIRS In your online course, you reflected on what situations in your life you would handle differently after studying more about building rapport. Discuss. Listen to the example.

B SHARE Present your ideas to the class.

VOCABULARY PRACTICE
Go to page 75.

I can explain work rapport and describe strategies for building and maintaining it. ☐

3

MODULE

Goal Setting

Strategic Career Goals

DISCUSSION STRATEGIES

Go to page 68.

Step 1 Get started

A Refresh your memory! Watch the *What You'll Learn* video.

B Look at the photo. What is the person's goal? Are they approaching that goal strategically and intentionally? How do you know? How is the picture a metaphor for career goal-setting?

C Check your understanding. Go to page 56.

Step 2 Tell your story

A THINK In your online course, you thought about a time you made a strategic goal at work, school, or in your personal life. What happened and what did you learn? Listen to the example.

B PAIRS Discuss your story.

C SHARE Tell your story to the class.

Step 3 Activate your knowledge

A PAIRS Listen and read each person's description of their current job or situation and what they hope to do in the future. Identify their long-term goals and their transferable skills.

My name is **Adriana**. I'm originally from Colombia, but I'm studying Law here in the U.S. and I work part-time in a restaurant. I have to memorize the list of different specials every day so that I can tell people about them. I'm lucky, the restaurant I work in is great, so people are usually in a good mood when they eat here. Sometimes customers aren't so nice, though. On busy nights they get annoyed for example, if I don't notice that their water glasses need to be re-filled. I try to stay positive anyway and this usually makes the customers happier, too. On some nights, the manager asks me to be the hostess, so I have to take reservations for people, greet them when they arrive, make sure they're on the list, and lead them to the right table. I have to make sure I remember all the details so that I don't make a mistake.

Recently, I've been thinking about getting into immigration law when I qualify. I meet a lot of people in my restaurant who have either immigrated from other countries, or who are just visiting but want to move here. But, it's really hard for them to figure out all of the details. There are forms to fill out, and every situation is unique. I really think that I would find it very satisfying if I could help them.

Long-term goal: ____________________

Transferable skills: ____________________

____

My name is **Mahir** and I'm a student. I'm doing a degree in education. When I'm at home, I spend my time studying. Once a week, I tutor high school kids, which I really love doing. When I was younger, school was very challenging for me because I have some learning difficulties. But I was taught some strategies to deal with them. Then I realized that what I learned is useful for everyone, not just for the kids with learning difficulties. So, when I tutor kids, I help them understand how to approach learning in general.

When I graduate next year, I'd like to get a job as a high school science teacher. Long-term, however, I'd really like to set up my own private after-school tutoring center. I don't think the traditional education system works for everybody. I'd like to use my personal experience to help kids—all kids—learn how to overcome any challenges so that they can learn more easily—and even develop a love of learning, like I did. In order to do this, I will eventually need to have a team of teachers who would want to work with me. And I would have to learn what's involved in setting up a school. But I really think I could do it if I set my mind to it.

Long-term goal: ____________________

Transferable skills: ____________________

____

B PAIRS Work together to identify three possible short-term goals for each person.

Possible short-term goals for Adriana:

1 This month ______________________

2 From September ______________________

3 Next year ______________________

Possible short-term goals for Mahir:

1 This month ______________________

2 From September ______________________

3 Next year ______________________

C SHARE Present your ideas to the class. Take notes while other pairs share their answers.

Step 4 Take away

GROUPS of 3–5 Think about the process you used to develop plans for the people in Step 3, as well as the information you learned in the online course. Complete the process timeline with the words in the box.

short-term goals	education or experience	transferable
SMART goals	interests	long-term	skills

1. Think about what your ______________ and ______________ are.
2. Identify your ______________ goal.
3. Identify your ______________ skills and consider how to develop them.
4. Consider what ______________ your long-term goal would require.
5. Create the ______________ that will take you toward your long-term goal.
6. Write your goals as ______________, creating a timeline for achieving them.

Step 5 Project

PAIRS In your online course, you interviewed someone who set strategic goals to achieve a career goal. Tell your partner what you learned. Read the example.

I interviewed my aunt, who owns her own clothing shop. She told me that she started out thinking she would be a fashion designer, but changed her mind when she realized how competitive it was. So, she changed her goal and decided to open a boutique. She had to take some business courses so that she knew what was involved in running a store. Then she found a retail job so that she could learn firsthand what it was like. She says that this is now her dream job.

Step 6 Talk!

GROUPS of 3–4 How do you figure out what your long-term goal is? Read the quotes and decide which strategy you think is best. Why? What other strategies can you come up with?

Mehmet Ali, ***Shooting Star Inc.***
"Personally, in order to come up with my own dream job, I needed to do a lot of thinking and reflect on what my deepest desire was. Think about what would make you really happy and what would be best suited to the skills you already have."

Emily Moore, ***Magnetic Solutions***
"I always tell people to write a letter from their 80-year-old self to their present-day self. In the letter, tell yourself what you achieved and what you are the most proud of doing in your life. This can really help people imagine their future selves more clearly."

Richard Thompson, ***The Bright Lights and Big City Company***
"I think the best way to think about your long-term goal is to ask yourself this question: What will you regret, if you don't do it during your life?"

Ju Yang, ***Wang and Wang Global Networks***
"Find a mentor that you can talk to, someone who has experience and wisdom. Share your ideas, your skills, your interests with them. Ask them to be honest and suggest what they think is possible for you to do. Their advice will be the most valuable thing for you."

Step 7 Going forward

A PAIRS In your online course, you reflected on how you will handle planning your career path differently after studying more about strategic career goals. Discuss. Listen to the example.

B SHARE Present your ideas to the class.

VOCABULARY PRACTICE Go to page 76.

I can explain the importance of strategic career goals and identify skills and steps to reach them. ☐

4

MODULE

Teamwork

Preventing and Managing Group Conflict

DISCUSSION STRATEGIES

Go to page 68.

Step 1 Get started

A Refresh your memory! Watch the *What You'll Learn* video.

B Look at the photo. This meeting isn't going well. What can the participants do to make the meeting go better?

C Check your understanding. Go to page 57.

Step 2 Tell your story

A THINK In your online course, you thought about a time you worked on a team or in a group that had a conflict. How did your team handle it? If you've never had a team conflict, what are some ways you've found to make groups work well together? Listen to the example.

B PAIRS Discuss your story.

C SHARE Tell your story to the class.

Step 3 Activate your knowledge

A PAIRS Kimiko has been assigned to manage a new team project. Read the email that she sent to her team. Check which conflict prevention strategies she used.

1

FROM: Kimiko Ayamoto
TO: Ben Numan, Laura Flinch, John Rivers

Dear Team,
I have spoken with each of you individually, and I hope you are as excited as I am to get started with our new project! Since I know you will all be bringing a lot of different ideas to the table, I would like to have an initial brainstorming meeting. So please jot down your ideas and come ready to share them! As we narrow down the ideas that we will work with, we can also use the time to figure out roles and responsibilities.

I will send a group calendar request for this initial meeting. Then we can determine a schedule that works for everyone for some regular status meetings.

Thanks,
Kimiko

- [ ] Communicate clearly and precisely.
- [ ] Maintain relationships.
- [ ] Respect others.
- [ ] Have a positive attitude.
- [ ] Listen to everyone's opinions.
- [ ] Stay calm.
- [ ] Don't blame others.
- [ ] Schedule regular meetings.

2 It is a month later. The team is having its first status meeting. Read and listen to part of the meeting. What happens during the meeting? Why? What conflict management strategies could the team have used to manage the situation?

Kimiko: Welcome to our first status meeting everyone. I'm so glad we finally managed to find a regular day and time that works for all of you. I appreciate you making the time for this. So, by now, I think you must have finished a lot of the initial research work, is that correct? Laura, do you want to start us off?

Laura: Sure. Well, I got some statistics from the sales team.

Ben: You did? I was waiting for those. Why didn't you send them to me?

Laura: Oh! I'm sorry, I didn't know you needed them, too.

Ben: Yeah, I did. Didn't you take notes during our last meeting?

Laura: As a matter of fact, yes. But you never said you needed those statistics.

John: (aside to Ben): Ben, actually, we talked about that. You were going to call Laura.

Ben: Really? I don't remember that.

Kimiko: Look, we all have the same goal here, and we need to keep moving forward. Let's just agree that Laura, you'll send Ben those statistics today. OK?

Laura: Sure. But next time Ben, just let me know if you're waiting for something, okay?

____

____

____

B PAIRS After the meeting, what do you think Kimiko and the other team members should do to follow up? How can they prevent future conflicts?

C SHARE Present your ideas to the class.

Step 4 Take away

GROUPS of 3–5 Create a diagram with conflict prevention and management tips. Use your notes from Step 3 as well as what you remember from your online course.

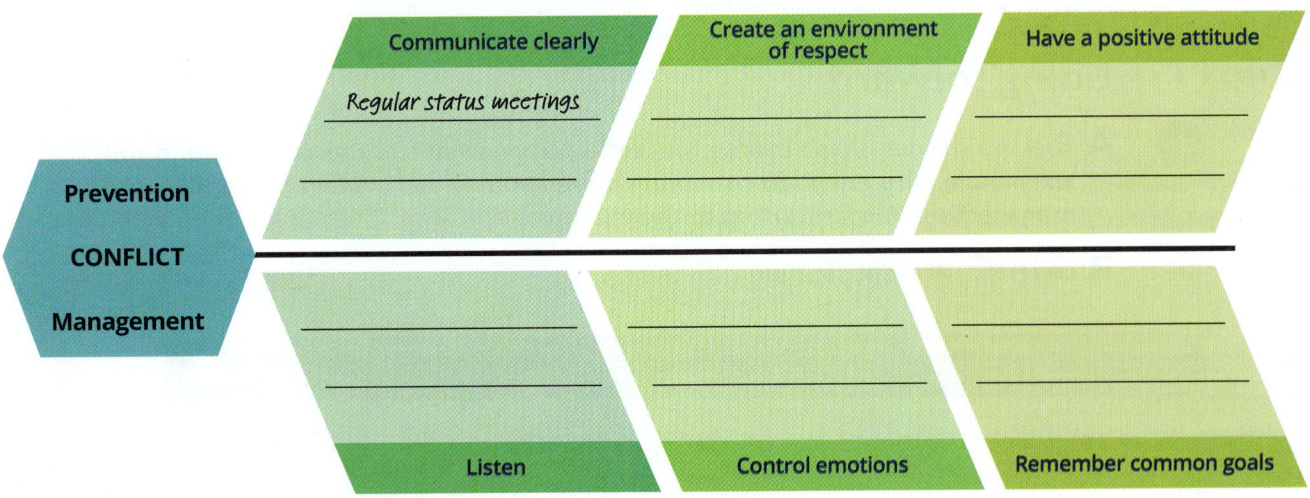

Step 5 Project

PAIRS In your online course, you interviewed three people about their conflict management strategies. Tell your partner what you learned. Read the example.

I talked to a friend of mine who is a high school teacher. I think he is really good at managing conflict because he has to work with teenagers every day, and they have strong opinions! He told me that creating a respectful environment on the first day of class is one of the most important things he does to prevent conflict.

Step 6 Talk!

PAIRS Complete the questionnaire and compare your answers with your partner's. Use the questions below to help guide your conversation.

1 It's easier to get ideas across in emails and messages than in face-to-face communication and you're less likely to be misinterpreted.	Agree Disagree
2 It's more difficult to discuss issues in a virtual meeting.	Agree Disagree
3 Conflict is more likely to occur on social media than in person.	Agree Disagree
4 Virtual communication is changing how we communicate in teams for the better.	Agree Disagree
5 It's more difficult to manage conflict in online and virtual situations.	Agree Disagree

Give reasons why you agree or disagree with the statements. Which type of online or virtual communication do you find easiest or most difficult? Why?

Step 7 Going forward

A PAIRS In your online course, you reflected on what situations in your life you will handle differently after studying more about group conflict prevention and management. Discuss. Listen to the example.

B SHARE Present your ideas to the class.

VOCABULARY PRACTICE Go to page 77.

I can explain causes of group conflict and describe strategies for preventing and managing conflict. ☐

5
MODULE

Critical Thinking

Evaluating Information

DISCUSSION STRATEGIES
Go to page 68.

Step 1 Get started

A Refresh your memory! Watch the *What You'll Learn* video.

B Look at the photo. What steps do you take to evaluate the information that you read or hear? Why is it important to do this?

C Check your understanding. Go to page 58.

Step 2 Tell your story

A THINK In your online course you thought about a time you evaluated information at work, school, or in your personal life. What happened and what did you learn? Listen to the example.

B PAIRS Discuss your story.

C SHARE Tell your story to the class.

Step 3 Take away

A PAIRS Review your notes from the online module. Then match the problems to the examples.

PROBLEMS	EXAMPLES
___ 1 Uses vague or incomplete language	a. "It was one of the most inspiring speeches ever given. Everyone who heard it shed tears."
___ 2 Uses emotional or absolute language	b. "Mr. Lane committed several armed robberies, but Ms Koons once shoplifted a candy bar. They're both criminals!"
___ 3 Uses information that is not up to date	c. "According to a survey of 12 university students, most professors assign too much homework."
___ 4 Does not cite sources	d. "A 2001 study found that more than 70% of teenagers use the internet."
___ 5 Makes false comparisons	e. "Thanks to my lucky socks, I won three races in a row!"
___ 6 Falsely claims something as a cause	f. "Critics say that the prime minister has lied many times about many things."
___ 7 Cites studies that don't meet standards	g. "I read that that the winning team cheated by letting air out of the ball."

B SHARE Check your answers with the class.

Step 4 Activate your knowledge

A THINK Read and evaluate the claims. What problems with credibility or logic does each claim have? Take notes.

1 A viral news story: "In an alarming incident over the weekend, a 23-year-old man became gravely ill after eating pizza from a local restaurant. The man reheated pizza that was left over from the previous night's dinner. Later that day, he became extremely sick and was taken to the hospital. The restaurant could not be reached for comment."

2 A study published in an academic journal: "According to a 2004 survey of 10 hiring managers, in-person training is better than online training for new employees. This is especially true for trainings on ethical behaviors in the workplace. These findings suggest that companies would benefit from developing face-to-face training workshops and materials for new employees."

3 A political commentator: "In her speech yesterday, Mayor Tripp criticized corporations for causing large amounts of air pollution through burning fuel. This is unfair because she drives an SUV, which also uses fuel and produces air pollution. Some people are saying that the only reason the Mayor gave that speech is because she accepted money for her re-election campaign from environmental organizations. It's clear that she doesn't really care about pollution!"

4 A product description on a company's website: "Our skincare products will make your skin feel softer and smoother than ever before! You'll love the dreamy scents and luxurious texture of our soaps and creams! Because we care about the environment, our products contain natural ingredients and our packaging is made with recycled materials."

B PAIRS Compare your notes with a partner. What steps could you take to evaluate each claim? What else can you do to make sure that you have accurate and reliable information about each topic? Make a list.

C SHARE Present your ideas to the class.

Step 5 Project

PAIRS **In your online course, you looked for a source of information about a subject and found three claims about it. Then you evaluated the credibility of each claim. Share the results of the evaluation with your partner. Read the example.**

I enjoy hiking in the mountains, so I listened to a podcast by a well-known hiking influencer about how to stay safe while hiking. I wrote down three claims:

1 "The National Hiking Association lists 10 essential items that you should always carry with you when you go hiking in order to stay safe."

2 "These safety tips are obvious to every experienced hiker, but it's amazing how many people make basic mistakes."

3 "Hiking can be dangerous. Every year, about 2,000 people get lost in the woods while hiking."

This first claim is credible. The number of items is specific, and the speaker cites a reliable source.

There are some problems with the second and third claims. For example, "every experienced hiker" is absolute language. The speaker also uses emotional language like "amazing" and "dangerous." Finally, the claim that 2,000 hikers get lost every year is incomplete without the total number of hikers. No source is provided. These claims might not be credible.

Step 6 Talk!

PAIRS **Discuss challenges around finding trustworthy sources for information or news. Use the facts and questions to help guide your conversation.**

65% **of people in Finland trust news media** compared to **36%** of people in the UK and **29%** in the U.S.

Globally, radio and television news is viewed as more dependable whereas social media is seen as less reliable.

177 **sites identified as false information websites attracted 14 million visits a month in the UK.**

The **majority** of respondents in a poll which included Brazil, India, and Nigeria felt that it would be appropriate for internet technology companies to display fact checking next to advertising, news links, and user posts.

- Should online platforms or governments do more to make sure that the information people share is credible or is it the responsibility of the individual to check?
- Where do you usually look for information or news? Do you think these sources are reliable? Why?
- Can you think of an example of false information that went viral? Why do you think it did?

Step 7 Going forward

A **PAIRS** **In your online course, you reflected on how the way you do your job or schoolwork will change after studying more about evaluating information. Discuss. Listen to the example.**

B **SHARE** **Present your ideas to the class.**

VOCABULARY PRACTICE
Go to page 78.

I can describe specific strategies for evaluating information. ☐

6 MODULE

Leadership

Building Leadership Skills

DISCUSSION STRATEGIES

Go to page 68.

Step 1 Get started

A Refresh your memory! Watch the *What You'll Learn* video.

B Look at the photo. What qualities do good leaders have? Are good leaders born or made?

C Check your understanding. Go to page 59.

Step 2 Tell your story

A THINK In your online course, you thought about a time you used leadership skills at work, school, or in your personal life. What happened and what did you learn? Listen to the example.

B PAIRS Discuss your story.

C SHARE Tell your story to the class.

Step 3 Take away

A PAIRS Review your notes from the online module and complete the chart with leadership skills from the box. Then add another skill to each section.

Motivate and inspire	Take risks	Work well with others	Make decisions	Empower others

______	______	______	______	______
• Have the confidence to step in when needed • Consider pros and cons • *Take responsibility for mistakes*	• Encourage collaboration • Respect others' views and opinions • ______	• Delegate responsibility • Trust others to make decisions • ______	• Have a vision and communicate it with others • Make people feel like part of something bigger • ______	• Challenge assumptions • Don't be afraid to make mistakes • ______

B SHARE Present your ideas to the class.

Step 4 Activate your knowledge

A PAIRS Read and discuss two letters from people looking for advice about difficult workplace situations. What leadership skills are needed in each situation? What skills could each manager improve?

1

Dear Workplace Whisperer,

My new employee is highly accomplished, and we were lucky to be able to hire her. She's very capable, but she seems to be having trouble integrating into our company and accepting how things work here. We manufacture medical supplies, and she has a lot of ideas for new ways of doing things. Her ideas are actually pretty good, but we already have policies and procedures in place. I've tried to explain that to her, but she keeps asking me to share her ideas with the senior management team. How can I help her to learn to stop trying to change things and just go with the flow?

Sincerely,
Company Man

2

Dear Workplace Whisperer,

I'm a manager at a publisher of children's books. I was excited to join the company because I believe strongly in their mission. Sometimes, though, it seems like short term concerns are more important than the mission. We're understaffed, and the team struggles to meet deadlines because we don't have enough people to do all the work. Management seems more concerned about saving money than with developing high-quality products. The team is incredibly stressed and unhappy. What can we do to improve morale and get everyone excited about working here again?

Sincerely,
Stressed and Depressed

B PAIRS Now read another letter. Discuss advice to give to the writer about how to handle the situation.

1

Dear Workplace Whisperer,

I was recently made the team lead for an important software development project. It's my first time leading a project team and I really want to do a good job. I wrote a detailed plan for how to complete the project. I gave everyone specific assignments and instructions, but the team is underperforming. To help out, I'm doing extra tasks myself. At first, everyone was excited about the project. Now, I'm overwhelmed, the rest of the team is unhappy, and the work isn't very good. I'm worried that if this project fails, I won't get another opportunity. What can I do to turn things around?

Sincerely,
Panicking Project Lead

C SHARE Present your ideas to the class.

Step 5 Project

PAIRS **In your online course, you researched a leader you admire to find ways they have shown leadership and what their leadership strengths are. Share your notes with your partner. Read the example.**

Nelson Mandela displayed several qualities that make a great leader. He inspired people with a vision for equality in South Africa. One of his strengths was his excellent communication skills and he gave speeches that motivated people to share his vision for a better future.

Mandela was willing to take risks. He was a partner in a law firm, and could have had a comfortable life. Instead, he became an activist. He famously spent 27 years in prison. He empowered people and listened carefully to the opinions of others, even if he disagreed with them.

Step 6 Talk!

PAIRS ***A board of directors* is a group of people that are chosen to manage a company's activities and success. Choose your own personal board of directors! Complete the chart with people who demonstrate each of the leadership skills you learned about. These can be famous people or people that you know. Then discuss your board of directors with your partner and answer the questions below.**

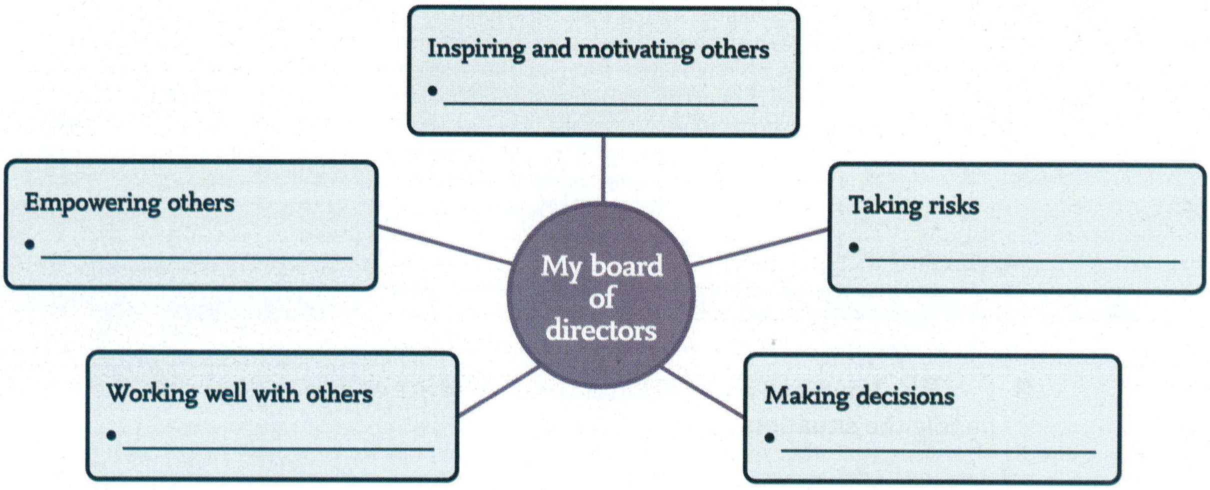

- Why did you choose each person? How does he or she demonstrate the skill in the circle?
- Which leadership skills do you have that would qualify you to sit on someone's board of directors?

Step 7 Going forward

A **PAIRS** **In your online course, you reflected on what situations in your work or personal life you could handle differently after studying more about leadership skills. Listen to the example.**

B **SHARE** **Present your ideas to the class.**

VOCABULARY PRACTICE Go to page 79.

I can describe the important skills of good leaders and strategies for good leadership. ☐

7

MODULE

Self-Management

Persistence

DISCUSSION STRATEGIES

Go to page 68.

Step 1 Get started

A Refresh your memory! Watch the *What You'll Learn* video.

B Look at the photo. What persistence skills do you think the people have developed to get to where they are?

C Check your understanding. Go to page 60.

Step 2 Tell your story

A THINK In your online course you thought about using persistence skills. Listen to the example.

B PAIRS Discuss your story.

C SHARE Tell your story to the class.

Step 3 Activate your knowledge

A PAIRS Listen to Asami, a caller to a radio show called "Best Business Advice on the Air!".

1 Which skills does Asami have? Which does she need to develop? Check (✓) the correct boxes.

Asami	Puts in continuous effort	Tries different strategies	Asks for help	Has a positive attitude
Has these skills				
Needs to develop these skills				

2 What would you suggest Asami do? Check (✓) as many suggestions as apply. Discuss your answers with a partner.

Suggestions for Asami

__Spend more time working.

__Rewrite her business plan.

__ Invite potential clients to lunch.

__Go to networking events for IT professionals.

__Give herself credit for finding three great software engineers who believe in her.

__Reach out to successful entrepreneurs and ask them how they made it.

B PAIRS Now listen to Pietro, another caller to the show.

1 Which skills does Pietro have? Which does he need to develop? Check (✓) the correct boxes.

Pietro	Puts in continuous effort	Tries different strategies	Asks for help	Has a positive attitude
Has these skills				
Needs to develop these skills				

2 What would you suggest Pietro do? Check (✓) as many suggestions as apply. Discuss your answers with a partner.

Suggestions for Pietro

___He needs to work harder.

___He needs to ask his boss for help.

___ He shouldn't let one obstacle stop him.

___He should make an appointment to talk to the senior director of operations.

___He might consider looking for a new job.

C SHARE Present your answers to A and B to the class.

Step 4 Take away

GROUPS of 3–5 Fill in the chart with two details for each main point. Include information from what you learned in the online course video *The Power of Yet*, your classmates, and your own ideas.

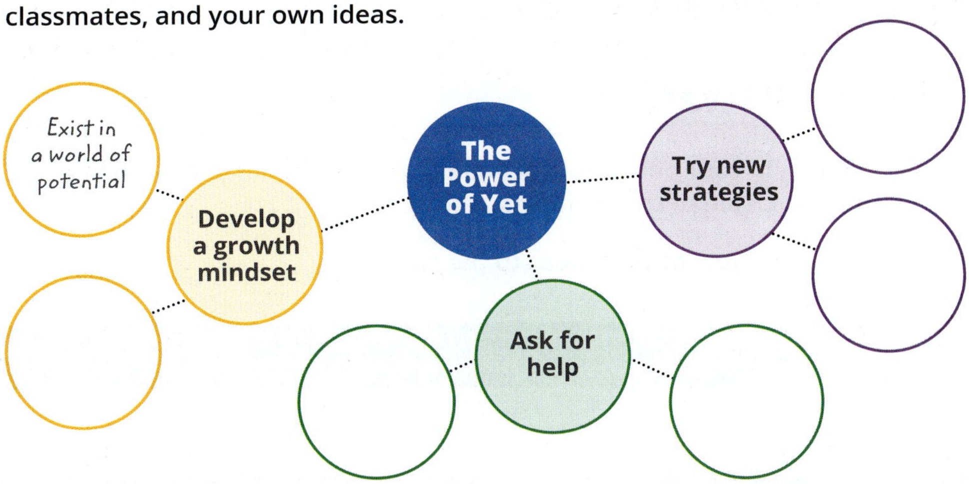

Step 5 Project

PAIRS In your online course you interviewed someone who had a positive attitude or who does not give up easily. Tell your partner about their strategies and solutions for persisting when they faced problems. Read the example.

My co-worker Jeannie told me that whenever she faces a challenge, she thinks of it as a learning opportunity. And since she loves learning, she gets excited by problems. So, it's easy for her to stay positive. She asks colleagues how they would handle the situation, and then tries one of their suggestions. If it doesn't work, she moves on to another strategy or searches online for an answer.

Step 6 Talk!

GROUPS of 3–5 Read the profiles of three famous people and discuss the questions.

Vera Wang, is a highly successful American fashion designer with a name that is recognized all over the world. However, many people do not know that before she got involved in fashion, she was a talented pairs figure skater who was expected to make the 1968 Olympics team. When she failed, she was devastated, but not long after began her highly successful career in fashion.

Albert Einstein, one of the most brilliant physicists of all time, with one of the highest IQs of anyone ever tested, was considered, at best, a mediocre student. He failed the exam to enter the Zurich polytechnic school when he was 15. He managed to pass the exam and was admitted to the school the following year but struggled and did not have an easy time graduating. After graduation he was unable to find a teaching job and instead began work as a clerk in a patent office. Obviously, those early academic struggles did not **deter** him. In 1921, at the age of 42, he won the Nobel Prize in Physics.

At the age of 13, **Bethany Hamilton**, a rising star in the world of surfing, lost one of her arms in a shark attack. Most people thought she would never surf again. But within two months she was back in the water, and two years later won her first national surfing title. Since then, she has won surf competitions all over the world. In 2018, she starred in an award-winning documentary about her life, "Unstoppable."

- What do all of these people have in common? What can we learn from them?
- Do you think you would have kept going if you faced these challenges? At what point would you have given up?
- Do you know any people, famous or not, who have succeeded after multiple failures? Tell your group about them.

Step 7 Going forward

A PAIRS In your online course you reflected on what you learned about persistence. Discuss. Listen to the examples.

B SHARE Present your ideas to the class.

VOCABULARY PRACTICE Go to page 80.

I can describe the importance of persistence and specific strategies to develop the *yet* attitude. ☐

8 MODULE

Wellness

Improving Wellness

DISCUSSION STRATEGIES
Go to page 68.

Step 1 Get started

A Refresh your memory! Watch the *What You'll Learn* video.

B Look at the photo. What are these people doing to improve their wellness? Which of these do you think is the hardest or easiest to do? Why?

C Check your understanding. Go to page 61.

Step 2 Tell your story

A THINK In your online course you thought about improving your wellness at school or at work. Listen to the example.

B PAIRS Discuss your story.

C SHARE Tell your story to the class.

Step 3 Activate your knowledge

A PAIRS Sarita is a wellness coach. All of her new clients complete a form about their habits during a typical week. Read one client's form. Write ✓ next to healthy habits, and X next to things that need improvement. Then add at least one more idea to each section to complete Sophie's Wellness Plan.

Better Living

Sarita Williams | Health and Wellness Coach

Client Name:	*Sophie Pulanski*	
Wellness Area	**Habits**	**Wellness Plan**
Physical activity	*Walk dog 2X a day for 15 min each – one 30 min walk 1X a week* *Sit a lot—at work and home* *Summer—much more active. Biking, tennis, swimming*	*In the winter, join a gym where you can swim and maybe play tennis.*
Diet	*Sweet tooth—cookies or ice cream every day* *Cook for myself—lots of veggies and fish* *Don't eat out much* *No time for lunch—usually just protein bar and soda at my desk*	*Cook extra for dinner and take the leftovers to work for lunch.*
Sleep	*Morning person up at 6—same schedule every day* *Check Social Media before bed* *6 hrs a night*	*Go to bed an hour earlier.*
Work or school	*Hate my job!!! Sit at a computer 9–5, M–F.* *Stressful—lots of deadlines. Don't know coworkers*	*Get to know people at work.*
Social activities/ relaxation	*Live alone, lonely sometimes* *TV, video games, social media at night during the week* *Meet a friend 1X a week to walk dogs together* *Chores all day Sat.* *Family on Sun.*	*Get together with friends on Saturday afternoon.*
Motivation	*Feel happier* *Have more energy* *Buy new clothes*	*Use a wall calendar to record steps toward your objectives and any successes.*
Goals	*Be more active* *Spend more time with friends and family* *Look for a new job*	*Think longer term about what kind of work you really want to do.*

B SHARE Share your ideas with a group. Add your classmates' ideas to your plan.

Step 4 Take away

GROUPS of 3–5 Match the examples to the correct categories in the chart. Discuss and write another suggestion to add to each category.

A Go online and research healthy food that you can use to replace unhealthy food that you're eating now.

B For one week, write down everything you do every day.

C Make a list of changes you want to make to your daily routine and put it somewhere where you will see it every day, for example on your bathroom mirror.

D Next to every day's activities, check the activities you want to continue doing, and write an X next to those you want to stop doing.

E Write down every healthy change you make, and reward yourself for each one.

F Next to every X on your list, write something you could do instead that would be healthier.

Evaluate daily routine ______ ______

____

Exchange unhealthy habits for healthier ones ______ ______

____

Ideas for staying motivated ______ ______

____

Step 5 Project

PAIRS In your online course you researched ways to improve your wellness using health tip websites, rather than personal blogs or websites that do not provide evidence for their claims. Then you wrote at least five healthy habits that you want to try to add to your routine. Read the example.

So, I decided to add one healthy habit to five areas of my life: work, free time, exercise, diet, and sleep. At work, I sit all the time staring at a computer screen. At the end of the day, I have a headache and my back is killing me. So now I set an alert on my phone, and once an hour I stand up to stretch, look out the window and take a short walk around the office. Getting up and moving, even just for a few minutes, makes me feel a lot better. In my free time, I realized I almost always do stuff indoors—video games, talking on the phone, streaming movies, eating in restaurants. I need some fresh air to clear my head! To get started, at least once a week I'm going to go outside instead—walk to the park or take a bike ride. Anything, as long as it's outdoors. That's also good exercise.

Step 6 Talk!

GROUPS of 3–5 Look at the pictures and read about wellness practices around the world. Discuss the questions.

Japan: Inemuri

The concept of Inemuri can be described in English as "sleeping while being present." This refers to the practice in Japan of taking short naps wherever you are, including at work. Unlike in many other countries, this practice is socially acceptable—even encouraged, in some cases. Japan is proud of its reputation as the "nation that never sleeps." At work, taking a short nap sends the signal that you work late hours and are therefore a very hard worker.

India: Laughing Yoga

Laughing yoga is a meditation practice developed by Indian doctor Madan Kataria. The practice is informed by scientific evidence that laughter is beneficial to your mental and physical health, and the brain does not distinguish between fake and real laughter. Laughing yoga involves movement and breathing exercises that are designed to result in intentional laughter. According to Dr. Kataria, the practice has numerous benefits, including lifting your mood, reducing stress, and strengthening your immune system.

South Africa and Zimbabwe: Ubuntu

The philosophy of Ubuntu, which is widespread in Southern Africa, particularly in South Africa and Zimbabwe, is complex. Put very simply, it is a philosophy that embraces the notion that human well-being is dependent on community members' sharing all community benefits and burdens equally. In short, Ubuntu involves putting the interests of the community before the interests of the individual.

Norway: Friluftsliv

An important part of Norweigan culture is the philosophy of friluftsliv. Friluftsliv stresses the importance to your overall health and well-being of spending time enjoying the outdoors. Friluftsliv includes any outdoor activity, from mountain climbing to spending an afternoon reading in a hammock. Friluftsliv is by far the most common leisure activity in Norway. It is more popular than all other sports and recreation activities combined.

- Have you tried any of these wellness practices? Are there any you would like to try?
- Which do you think could be useful in the workplace? Why?
- Do you know any other wellness practices which could help health, happiness or wellbeing?

Step 7 Going forward

A **PAIRS** In your online course you learned about how to improve your wellness. Discuss. Listen to the examples.

B **SHARE** Present your ideas to the class.

VOCABULARY PRACTICE
Go to page 81.

I can explain the habits and importance of wellness and describe specific strategies for improving it. ☐

9

MODULE

Social Responsibility

Giving Back

DISCUSSION STRATEGIES

Go to page 68.

Step 1 Get started

A Refresh your memory! Watch the *What You'll Learn* video.

B Look at the photo. How are the people giving back to their community? What do you think is their motivation?

C Check your understanding. Go to page 62.

Step ② Tell your story

A THINK In your online course you thought about a time that you gave back. Listen to the example.

B PAIRS Discuss your story.

C SHARE Tell your story to the class.

Step ③ Activate your knowledge

A PAIRS Listen to three callers on a talk show called, "How Can I Help?". You'll hear the caller, but not the host's reply. For each caller, take notes about their situation.

Speaker	Position and Situation	Goal(s)	Suggestions
Jacek 			
Ariane 			
Dwayne 			

B PAIRS Compare your answers. Then write some suggestions you think the host would make.

C SHARE Share your answers with the class.

Step 4 Take away

GROUPS of 3–5 **Complete the spidergram with the information in the box.**

build	companies	important	join
not working	résumé	start	working

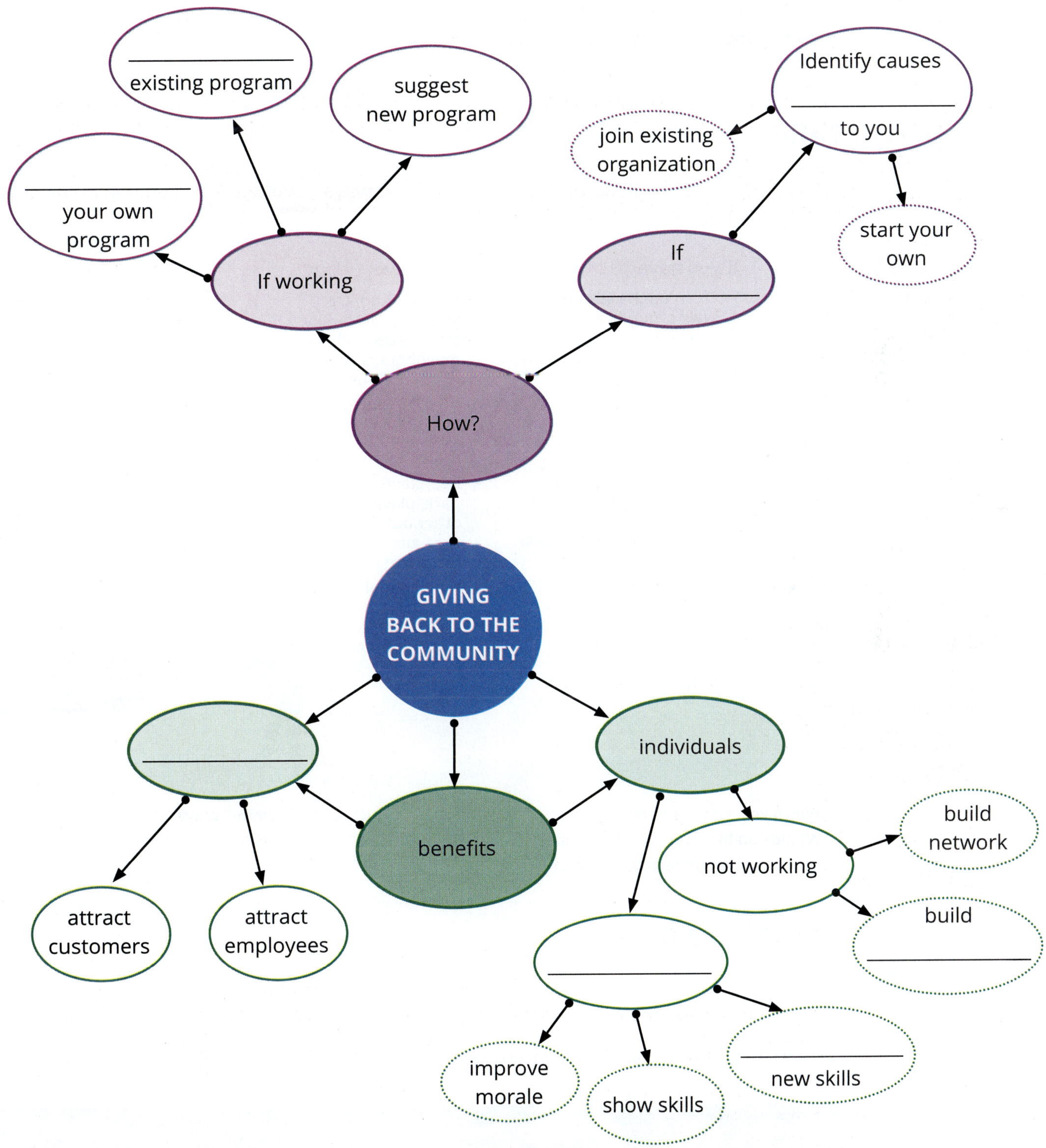

Step 5 Project

PAIRS In your online course you interviewed someone about how they give back or researched volunteer opportunities. What did you learn and how could you use what you learned? Read the example.

I researched volunteer opportunities in my seaside community. I'm concerned about the oceans, so I searched for environmental groups that work to protect the ocean. I found a program that needs volunteers to help clean up the beaches. People can just sign up on their website. So, I'm going to help them out every Saturday. My research has made me aware of how much is going on in just my area. Now that I know this, I've promised myself that wherever I live, I'll find a way to give back to the community.

Step 6 Talk!

GROUPS of 3–5 Read the suggestions about ways to volunteer if you don't have a lot of time. Then answer the questions.

If you have **5 minutes...**

- Save water: Make your friends a five-minute playlist to listen to while they shower so that they know they need to get out of the shower when the playlist ends.
- Collect clothing to donate to a homeless shelter: Clean out a drawer or a small part of your closet and set aside clothes you can donate.
- Repost an article on a cause you believe in to your social media accounts.
- Support a friend or family member: Record and send a supportive message to a friend or family member who is having a hard time.

If you have **30 minutes...**

- Clean up the streets: Walk around your neighborhood and pick up trash.

- Contact your local representatives: Write an email to your local representatives encouraging them to support a cause you believe in.

If you have **1 hour...**

- Donate food: Call your friends, family, classmates and neighbors and ask them to donate one **non-perishable** food item. Then pick up the items and take them to the food bank.
- Recycle: Go to a local park, playground, or other outdoor recreation area and collect cans and bottles to recycle.
- Help animals: Go to your local animal shelter and volunteer to walk a dog.

If you have **1 day...**

- Feed the hungry: Work one day a week at a food pantry.
- Help the elderly:
  - Visit a local senior care center to talk or read aloud to the residents
  - Deliver meals to the elderly in your community.

- Which volunteer opportunity interests you the most? Which is most useful? Why?
- Would you like to try any of the ideas above? Which one(s)?
- Have you ever done any volunteer work? What did you do?

Step 7 Going forward

A PAIRS In your online course you thought about giving back. Discuss. Listen to the example.

B SHARE Present your ideas to the class.

VOCABULARY PRACTICE Go to page 82.

I can explain the importance of social responsibility and describe ways to give back. ☐

10 MODULE

Branding

Branding Yourself Online

DISCUSSION STRATEGIES
Go to page 68.

Step 1 Get started

A Refresh your memory! Watch the *What You'll Learn* video.

B Look at the photo. How can you build your brand online?

C Check your understanding. Go to page 63.

Step 2 Tell your story

A THINK In your online course you thought about a time your online brand made a difference in your work, school, or personal life. Listen to the example.

B PAIRS Discuss your story.

C SHARE Tell your story to the class.

Step 3 Activate your knowledge

A PAIRS Andre Williams is a real estate agent. Look at Andre's social media accounts and check the aspects he has included.

ProContact

Andre Williams
Realtor
Trenton, NJ

500+ connections
DreamHomesRealty
Coleman Community College

ABOUT Licensed realtor, buyer's agent. My goal is to bring together buyers and sellers and ensure a smooth process from start to finish. I specialize in first-time home buyers, guiding you through all of the steps that can make homebuying overwhelming. I'll take care of the details. You focus on finding your dream home!

EXPERIENCE	DreamHomesRealty, 2019–present
EDUCATION	AD in Business Administration, Coleman Community College 2018
LICENSES AND CERTIFICATIONS	Licensed real estate agent in state of New Jersey
MEMBERSHIPS	Member of North East Surfers club 2012–present
AWARDS	1st place winner, East Coast Surf Competition, 2020 Buyer's agent of the year, 2020
VOLUNTEERING	New Jersey Affordable Housing Services (2017–present)

SurferBoy98@Friendsbook.com

Friendsbook

SurferBoy98
250 buddies

Trenton, NJ
AndreWilliams@DreamHomesReality.com

born Aug. 30, 1998
Joined 2019

About
Full time surfing fanatic and sell real estate in my free time! 🙂 Serously, I'm a realter with a passion for helpping fist-time home buyers make there dreams come true. If your looking for help finding new home then contact me at the link below and I'll get right back to you (as soon as I've finished at the gym or catching waves on the beach lol!)

March 2019

Andre Williams
Just got my realter's lisense! Already hooked up with DreamHomesRealty.com SWEET!!!

Bill Baxter
☹ No more time for waves?

Andre Williams
No wories, man—Surfing'll always be my main job. 🙂

♡ 25

B PAIRS How can Andre fix the mistakes in his social media accounts?

	ProContact	Friendsbook
PROFESSIONAL		
ENTHUSIASTIC		
HEALTH AND FITNESS		
APPROPRIATE EXPERIENCE		
ATTENTION TO DETAIL		
FRIENDLY		

C SHARE Share your answers with the class.

Step 4 Take away

GROUPS of 3–5 **Here are some common mistakes that people make when building a brand. Write the letter of a category next to each mistake.**

Categories

a. Be professional and pay attention to detail
b. Keep your private information private
c. Tell a story about yourself
d. Keep profiles up-to-date

Mistakes

_____ 1. You have not restricted who can see what on your social media page.

_____ 2. You got a new job a year ago. You haven't added your new job to your experience on your professional social media account.

_____ 3. Your username for all of your social media accounts is *partytime20*.

_____ 4. Your professional social media page shows no enthusiasm for your work or information about your personality.

_____ 5. You use your full name on your personal social media account which includes pictures of you partying.

_____ 6. Your personal website has several spelling mistakes.

Step 5 Project

PAIRS In your online course you interviewed two people with a strong, successful online presence. Read the example.

One person advised me that since I'm working now, I should definitely provide links to my employer and share positive articles about them on my job networking site. She also mentioned how important it is to make sure I understand the privacy settings on all my social media accounts and to remember to check and update them frequently. And I should still be careful about what I post, avoiding anything controversial or political. I was really surprised when she told me it's possible for someone to get around privacy settings if they're good with computers.

Step 6 Talk!

PAIRS Read and discuss each of the facts. Does any fact especially surprise you?

5% of job seekers say they didn't get a job because one of their potential employers was put off by something in their social media profiles.

85% of millennial job seekers use social media to search for jobs.

91% of employers use social media in their hiring process.

87% of job seekers update a social media profile before submitting job applications.

73% of millennials found their last job on a social media platform.

10% of job seekers have created social media posts to attract employers.

14% of job seekers change their social media accounts' privacy settings to prevent potential employers from finding their accounts.

Step 7 Going forward

A PAIRS In your online course you thought about branding online. Discuss. Listen to the example.

B SHARE Present your ideas to the class.

VOCABULARY PRACTICE Go to page 83.

I can describe strategies for developing my personal online brand. ☐

11

MODULE

Job Search

How to Research Companies

DISCUSSION STRATEGIES

Go to page 68.

Step 1 Get started

A Refresh your memory! Watch the *What You'll Learn* video.

B Look at the photo. The person is looking at the website for a company he might want to work for. What information might he hope to find about the company?

C Check your understanding. Go to page 64.

Step 2 Tell your story

A THINK In your online course you thought about a time when you researched something important for work, school, or for your personal life. Listen to the example.

B PAIRS Discuss your story.

C SHARE Tell your story to the class.

Step 3 Activate your knowledge

A 

PAIRS Carrie, a career advisor, meets with three different clients. They are at different stages in the process of finding and researching companies where they might like to work. Listen and complete the chart. Check the steps Carrie's clients have already taken.

Already done	Paul	Himari	Elena
1 chosen companies in locations where they want to live			
2 decided what is important to them when choosing a company			
3 looked at a company's website			
4 found a contact at one of the companies to talk to			
5 found information about a company's culture			
6 found financial information about a company			
7 found information about salary			

B PAIRS Read Carrie's advice and put the name of the client—Paul, Himari, or Elena—in the speech bubble.

1 Hi, ____________. You could look at more sections of the company's website.

2 Hello, ____________. Why don't you check out their social media account? They might list events they're hosting or involved with.

3 Hey, ____________. It sounds like we need to review what's most important to you in terms of location

C SHARE What additional advice would you give? Present your answers to the class.

1 **Paul** ______________________________

____

2 **Himari** ______________________________

____

3 **Elena** ______________________________

____

Step 4 Take away

GROUPS of 3–5 Answer the questions about researching companies.

1 How can you find out about a company's priorities and values?

____

2 How can you connect with somebody who works at a company?

____

3 How can you find out what employees like and dislike about working for a company?

____

4 How can you find out if a company is having any events that you could attend?

____

5 Where can you find out what products and services a company offers?

____

6 Where can you find out if there are opportunities at a company that weren't posted on an employment site?

____

7 Where can you find a job that matches your skills and qualifications?

____

8 If you are qualified for a lot of jobs in your field, how can you narrow your job search?

____

Step 5 Project

PAIRS In your online course you chose a company that you would like to know more about and did some research about the company, making a list of pros and cons. Share your findings with your partner. Read the example.

I researched a small business consulting company. The first thing I learned was that the research takes a lot of time! But after finishing the project, I know how to find a company that's a good fit for where I'm at in my career. And that's a great feeling!

Ok, so here are a couple of pros about the company I researched. Their mission statement touched on things that are very important to me: work/life balance, independence, and diversity. And their salaries compare well to other companies

On the con side, several people who work there posted on job review sites that the work environment isn't great—they mentioned the offices needed updating, and there aren't very many windows. Another con is that their benefits aren't so great. They only offer two-weeks of vacation at first—and it takes two years to get another week! So I wasn't crazy about that.

Step 6 Talk!

PAIRS There are several key areas to look at when looking for a job. Read the information and decide how you would number each item in order of priority for yourself.

___ **What is the staff turnover?** The number one reason for people leaving a company seems to be salary. But just behind that is the lack of opportunities for career development.

___ **How successful is the company?** This isn't just about financial performance. Just as importantly, companies that are seen to be performing well are those that also make the news for other matters, such as how well they treat they employees.

___ **Is there a good work-life balance?** Use social networking to see if any of your connections work, or used to work, for the company. Find out everything you can about how the company treats its employees. Does it genuinely care for their physical and mental health?

___ **Do you fit in?** In an interview, asking about a company's ethics or what they expect from their employees are just some of the questions that can give you an idea of whether you will fit on or not. If the answers don't match with what you are looking for, there's no point pretending otherwise.

___ **What can you learn?** Progressing in your career isn't just about a new job title and more responsibility. Will you be able to develop your skills and become more employable in the market, as a whole?

___ **Is there a point?** Apart from just paying the bills and supporting your lifestyle, will you have a sense of purpose at your job? How important is it for you to feel a sense of pride in what you do or to know that you are making a difference?

Step 7 Going forward

A PAIRS In your online course you thought about researching companies. Discuss. Listen to the example.

B SHARE Present your ideas to the class.

VOCABULARY PRACTICE
Go to page 84.

I can describe the benefits of and specific strategies for researching companies during the job-search process. ☐

12 MODULE

Interviewing

Answering Difficult Questions

DISCUSSION STRATEGIES

Go to page 68.

Step 1 Get started

A Refresh your memory! Watch the *What You'll Learn* video.

B Look at the photo. What do you think is happening? How do you think the woman feels? Why?

C Check your understanding. Go to page 65.

Step 2 Tell your story

A THINK In your online course you thought about a time when you were being interviewed for school admissions or a job. Listen to the example.

B PAIRS Discuss your story.

C SHARE Tell your story to the class.

Step 3 Activate your knowledge

A PAIRS Listen to excerpts from four interviews. Answer the questions at the end of each interview.

1

What did Jared do well?

- ○ **a.** He sounded very positive about what he did during his **gap year**.
- ○ **b.** He explained how his travel experiences relate to this job.
- ○ **c.** He kept his answers brief and to the point.

What mistake did Jared make?

- ○ **a.** He didn't sound sincere when he was talking about his travel experiences.
- ○ **b.** He wasn't prepared to answer an obvious question.
- ○ **c.** He got upset when the interviewer asked him a difficult question.

2

What did Melanie do well?

- ○ **a.** She gave a good reason for applying for the job.
- ○ **b.** She made a connection between her landscaping job and her major in college.
- ○ **c.** She sounded very enthusiastic about starting a new job.

What mistake did Melanie make?

- ○ **a.** She didn't answer one of the interviewer's questions.
- ○ **b.** She wasn't well prepared to answer why she was applying for the job.
- ○ **c.** She said something negative about her previous employer.

3

What did Liz do well?

◯ **a.** She showed the interviewer that she was passionate about her career.

◯ **b.** She did a good job handling a difficult question about her lack of experience.

◯ **c.** She spoke very honestly about a negative experience she had at one of her jobs.

What mistake did she make?

◯ **a.** She shouldn't have put so many jobs on her résumé.

◯ **b.** It wasn't necessary for her to be so negative about one of her jobs.

◯ **c.** She wasn't prepared for the interviewer's questions.

B PAIRS Listen to the interviews again. What did you learn from these that will help you improve your interviewing skills?

C SHARE Share your answers in a small group.

Step 4 Take away

GROUPS of 3–5 Discuss the questions and write your own answers.

What would you do if the interviewer asked about ...	
1. a skill that you don't have?	______
2. why you have had so many jobs or why there are gaps in your employment record?	______
3. how you would handle a situation that's specific to their organization?	______
4. a job that you were fired from or a job or employer that you strongly disliked?	______
5. something obvious that you forgot to prepare an answer for?	______

Step 5 Project

PAIRS In your online course you did a search on difficult interview questions and answered the questions based on your own experience, using the tips that you learned. Read the example. Share your questions and answers with your partner.

I found one question that was really strange—If you were stranded on a desert island, and you had only three things with you, what would you want them to be? Explain your answers.

I said I would like to have my dog, a fishing pole, and a knife. My dog because he is very good company—I never get sick of spending time with him. My fishing pole so that I would be able to feed us, and a knife because it would be useful for lots of stuff, like cutting down branches or small trees to make a shelter. I shared my answers with my brother and he thought my answers showed that I am practical and creative.

Step 6 Talk!

GROUPS of 3–5 Read and discuss the facts. Use the questions to guide your discussion.

Interview Behavior	Percentage of employers who identified the behavior as the worst
lying	68.5%
arriving late	65.3%
not appearing neat and clean	29.6 %
talking about other interviews or job offers	17.8%
not making eye contact	16.9%
not being dressed appropriately	15.5%
being sarcastic	14.6%
being too reserved and not showing your personality	4.7 %

based on a survey of over 300 UK employers

- Which information is the most interesting? Why?
- Which three behaviors do you think are worst? Why?
- Have you or anyone you know ever made one of these mistakes? Tell your group about it.

Step 7 Going forward

A PAIRS In your online course you thought about answering difficult interview questions. Listen to the example.

B SHARE Present your ideas to the class.

VOCABULARY PRACTICE
Go to page 85.

I can describe strategies for answering both common and difficult interview questions. ☐

CHECK YOUR UNDERSTANDING

Check your understanding 1

REFRESH YOUR MEMORY! Review the Online Course material in your Resources.

Choose the best answers. More than one answer may be correct in some items.

1 **What are the three parts of active listening?**
- **a** Making eye contact, understanding, non-verbal responses.
- **b** Engaging, focusing, reacting.
- **c** Comprehending, retaining, responding.

2 **Active listening lets you ____.**
- **a** build better relationships
- **b** create good work situations
- **c** finish meetings more quickly

3 **Making eye contact shows the speaker ____.**
- **a** you are in charge of the situation
- **b** you are paying attention
- **c** you are trying to remember what was said

4 **What can you do to show you are listening respectfully?**
- **a** Finish the speaker's sentences to show you are paying attention.
- **b** Use body language like tapping your fingers to show you want to speak.
- **c** Wait until it is your turn to speak, and repeat what others have said.

5 **Paula and Anada are talking online and discussing the new computer system. Paula is often looking down to take notes, and Anada is doing most of the talking. Anada feels like Paula is not listening to her. Why does Anada feel this way?**
- **a** Paula did not tell Anada she would be taking notes.
- **b** Anada thinks Paula is doing other work.
- **c** Anada thinks Paula should ask questions to clarify.

6 **Tye is in a meeting with other teachers. They are talking about the details for the big school trip next week. Everyone is nodding and sometimes asking questions. What does this show?**
- **a** They are paying attention.
- **b** They agree with everything the other teachers are saying.
- **c** They want to understand the ideas being discussed.

7 **Matteo is at a presentation at his company about how to volunteer to help schoolchildren with their homework. Some of the presenter's points are unclear. What can Matteo do to make sure he understands?**
- **a** When it is time for questions, say the ideas in his own words to confirm the meaning.
- **b** Finish some of the presenter's sentences to check the main ideas.
- **c** Interrupt the presentation and ask questions so that everyone understands.

8 **Shery is a new receptionist at a hair salon. Nancy is explaining how to include customers' payments in the computer system. Nancy knows the system is difficult because the payments need to be recorded for each stylist, and she feels like Shery is not paying attention. What could Shery be doing that makes Nancy feel this way?**
- **a** Shery could be looking up at the clock to check the time.
- **b** Shery could be using her own words to ask a few questions.
- **c** Shery could be checking her email and texts while listening.

Check your understanding 2

REFRESH YOUR MEMORY!

Review the Online Course material in your Resources.

Choose the best answers. More than one answer may be correct in some items.

1 Rapport is when co-workers ____.

- **a** become great friends
- **b** have friendly agreement
- **c** try to understand each other

2 Building rapport ____.

- **a** takes energy, so it decreases productivity
- **b** creates good working situations
- **c** builds trust between people

3 To maintain rapport, you should ____.

- **a** respect others whenever you interact with them
- **b** offer help or support
- **c** ask specific questions that are easy to respond to

4 Which statements demonstrate ways to support others?

- **a** Ask a co-worker if he needs help.
- **b** Wait to answer a customer's request until you are not busy.
- **c** Use creativity to discover how to help a client.

5 Dr. Amina Tal is a dentist. She is interviewing Lucas to work as a receptionist in her dental office. What should Lucas do to create a good first impression?

- **a** Smile and introduce himself.
- **b** Look away as they shake hands.
- **c** Address her by her name as they talk.

6 Tito recently started working as a graphic artist. He is nervous because he has a lot to learn. He met Emi, his co-worker, during the job interview last month. Tito and Emi meet in the parking lot and walk together to their office building. What can Tito do to build rapport?

- **a** Talk about unimportant things so they get to know each other more.
- **b** Ask Emi about her salary and how often she gets a raise.
- **c** Find some common interests so they feel more comfortable

7 Noomi is in her company's conference room holding a status update meeting with her team. The team is giving her statistics and information about the popularity of their new internet commercial. What should Noomi do to show openness to the team?

- **a** Nod sometimes.
- **b** Look and smile at each speaker.
- **c** Cross her arms across her chest.

8 Eric and May are sales managers. They are in an online meeting with their team to discuss strategies to increase sales. Eric makes a few suggestions that May does not agree with. What should May do to disagree but maintain rapport?

- **a** Interrupt Eric and share her ideas so they save time.
- **b** Ask questions to better understand his ideas.
- **c** Consider how to combine Eric's ideas with hers.

Check your understanding 3

REFRESH YOUR MEMORY!
Review the Online Course material in your Resources.

Choose the best answers. More than one answer may be correct in some items.

1 **Who needs to have strategic career goals?**
- **a** only people who want to change jobs
- **b** only people who want to find their dream jobs
- **c** people at all stages of their careers

2 **Why do you need strategic career goals?**
- **a** They help you control your career path.
- **b** They help you make choices so you can grow and develop.
- **c** They help you dream about things that seem impossible.

3. **You should think about ____ and then set your long-term goal to get your dream job.**
- **a** the things you can do
- **b** the salary and benefits
- **c** the things you like to do

4 **Why should you talk to your manager when you are interested in a new career goal?**
- **a** to tell the manager you are planning to change jobs and will be quitting
- **b** to see if there are opportunities to learn new skills within your company
- **c** to explain your new timeline to the manager so she understands your situation

5 **Yu is a bookkeeper, but he wants to be a licensed accountant. He wrote down several short-term goals, including:**

Take a tax accounting class this fall.

Sign up for the exam in May of next year. If I don't pass this exam, I cannot get a license.

Why is it important to write these goals?
- **a** so his goals are not too small
- **b** so he will remember he is SMART
- **c** so he can change the goals if necessary

6 **Samira works at a nail salon. She loves meeting people and taking care of their nails, but recently, she has been thinking she would like to own her own salon. She is worried because she knows she must take some classes to learn how to run a business. Samira's friend owns his own salon, so Samira asks for advice. What should the friend say?**
- **a** "Your new goal isn't far from your original job."
- **b** "You'll have to start over again, so you should think a little more."
- **c** "You already have some of the skills, which will help you in your new role."

7 **Maya leads a team of real estate agents, and she also sells real estate. As part of her job, she talks with others over the phone, on Zoom, and in person. She thinks quickly and responds to clients' concerns and questions. She finds original ways to solve problems. She wants to become a teacher. Which skills can she transfer to being an elementary school teacher?**
- **a** good communication
- **b** ability to be creative
- **c** knowledge of how to sell things

8 **Yonas thinks he has a great job as an Emergency Medical Technician. He loves riding in the ambulance to respond to emergency calls and help others, but he wants to try something new by becoming a Physician Assistant. To re-align his goals and make a career plan, what should he do?**
- **a** Start an internship to get experience in the new field.
- **b** Identify the skills he has that will be helpful in his new job.
- **c** Start looking for a new job as soon as possible.

Check your understanding 4

REFRESH YOUR MEMORY!
Review the Online Course material in your Resources.

Choose the best answers. More than one answer may be correct in some items.

1 Conflict can be caused by and escalate because of ____.

a differences in ways of thinking
b a lack of communication
c clear expectations

2 To prevent conflict, ____.

a first focus on the big problems rather than the small ones
b use email so people have more time to think
c explain end goals when starting a project

3 To create a respectful environment, ____.

a encourage diversity through many opinions
b do not allow disagreement about core company ideas
c give everyone what they need for success

4 How can you create an atmosphere of trust and respect?

a Help everyone feel comfortable to disagree with you.
b Keep repeating your opinion so it is clear to everyone.
c Listen to other people's ideas so they feel heard.

5 Ly-Kim and her team are creating a new internet commercial for a client. The team members are working remotely, and they do not meet in person to discuss the project. What can she do to prevent conflict?

a Hold regular status meetings and encourage everyone to talk about their concerns.
b Wait to explain responsibilities so team members do not feel pressure at the beginning.
c Build extra days into the schedule so they can better respond to delays.

6 Da-bin is the head personal trainer at a gym. There are four other trainers, and they are gathering in the meeting room to discuss new ways to encourage clients who have not been coming to the gym to come back. As the trainers enter the room, Da-bin makes small talk and says something each of them has recently done well. How do these actions help prevent conflict?

a She is creating positive team relationships.
b She is promoting diversity of ideas for the workplace.
c She is acknowledging their work and creating high morale.

7 Rita sells real estate. She is in her manager's office discussing last quarter's sales, which were not as strong as they had hoped. Her manager is blaming Rita, and Rita wants to explain why her sales were lower than they expected. What should Rita do?

a Take a moment to control her feelings.
b Be respectful as she discusses the situation.
c Calmly tell the manager he is being impatient.

8 Solomon is a manager at a company that organizes educational trips to other countries during the summer. His team did not sign up as many students as other teams, so they are in his office talking about the problem. Which statements should Solomon use to help prevent and manage conflict?

a "You should have listened to the advice I gave you two months ago."
b "You missed your goals. What mistakes do you think you made?"
c "Let's brainstorm how we can learn from last quarter's problems."

Check your understanding 5

REFRESH YOUR MEMORY! Review the Online Course material in your Resources.

Choose the best answers. More than one answer may be correct in some items.

1 You should evaluate information so that you ____.

a make wise decisions

b make sure you have many sources

c can decide whether you agree

2 To know whether information is reliable, you need to ____.

a check whether the source is a respected authority

b consider whether claims are facts, opinions, or in between

c examine how useful it is for you

3 To evaluate whether a claim is a fact or an opinion, you should ____.

a examine how much evidence supports it

b check whether the evidence is credible

c see whether the evidence is written in understandable English

4 When you think about the credibility of a claim, you make sure it ____.

a includes evidence to support it

b uses language that influences emotion

c does not have incomplete or vague statements

5 Evidence should ____.

a be reasonably up-to-date

b come from sources that are only slightly biased

c include accurate sources that you can verify

6 You read some official city documents that showed the city is thinking about increasing taxes, but has not yet decided whether to do so. That same morning, you watched an online news story, and the reporter said, "This is so disappointing. The city is once again increasing taxes, this time to build a parking lot that we don't even need." How would you evaluate this story?

a There is a lack of credibility because of emotional language.

b There are changes from the original sources.

c The story is out of date.

7 You are reading a travel company's travel brochure.

Come to the islands! They have the best food in the world, and they are one of the cheapest places in the area to stay on your next vacation.

How would you evaluate these claims?

a The claims are not supported.

b The claims are too vague.

c The claims give measurable details.

8 You sell winter coats at a store, and this year's sales were much better than last year's. You are in a meeting, discussing the reasons why sales were so good. During the meeting, salespeople and the manager gave these ideas. Which are false comparisons?

a People traveled more this year.

b Beach clothes sales were up this year, too.

c Competitor's coat sales were also higher than last year.

9 You work in Human Resources in a large company. In a study, you read, "Employees who work longer hours are more loyal to the company than employees who work only 40 hours a week. Therefore, working longer hours must cause employees to be loyal." How would you evaluate this statement?

a There is no problem because there is only one outcome.

b It is possible that the employees who work longer are already more loyal.

c There may be another factor that causes both outcomes.

10 You are a community health worker. You are reading a study about the health of five high school students in one school in your city. What conclusions can you make about the study?

a The study was done properly.

b The number of students was too small.

c The sample is not biased.

Check your understanding 6

REFRESH YOUR MEMORY!
Review the Online Course material in your Resources.

Choose the best answers. More than one answer may be correct in some items.

1 **To be an effective leader, you need to be able to ____.**
- **a** make sure the right person does each job
- **b** force your views once in a while
- **c** step back and let others do their best

2 **When they want to challenge assumptions, leaders need to ____.**
- **a** make sure that mistakes are avoided
- **b** show others how to do things better
- **c** be confident even when others resist

3 **To make decisions, a good leader must ____.**
- **a** only consider the cons of the decision
- **b** be willing to take risks
- **c** delegate both work and decision-making

4 **Good leaders have to ensure accountability for mistakes so that they do not happen again. What strategies do good leaders use when dealing with mistakes?**
- **a** They help other people learn from them.
- **b** They are not afraid to admit their own mistakes.
- **c** They publicly announce who makes mistakes.

5 **Ari started a company to make phone apps, and he has recently hired his first three employees. What skills and strategies should he use to be an effective leader?**
- **a** Explain his vision for the company clearly so his employees are excited.
- **b** Explain that he is very busy so they should help each other with problems.
- **c** Help them feel like they are part of something more than just a job.

6 **Sandy was recently transferred to a different insurance office and became the manager. She noticed the employees do not work well together as a team. What leadership strategies can she use to increase collaboration?**
- **a** Create an atmosphere where ideas are respected.
- **b** Make sure everyone is treated fairly.
- **c** Try to do everything so she models hard work.

7 **Azam manages a group of security guards. Every hour, he checks his computer monitor to make sure the guards are doing their job well. The guards must check with him before they make any decisions. At the end of the week, he meets with each of them privately and tells them what they are doing wrong. How could he be a more effective leader?**
- **a** Trust them to do their work, and not micromanage them.
- **b** Suggest ways to improve, but acknowledge their good points.
- **c** Explain their problems publicly so they accept responsibility.

8 **Asim is a captain in a fire station. He is training a firefighter who will then move to another station and be the head firefighter. He is explaining about how to handle mistakes. What strategies are important?**
- **a** Create an atmosphere where people admit their mistakes.
- **b** For big accomplishments, give praise in front of others.
- **c** Create an atmosphere where everyone comments on others' mistakes.

Check your understanding 7

REFRESH YOUR MEMORY! Review the Online Course material in your Resources.

Choose the best answers. More than one answer may be correct in some items.

1 **What is persistence?**

The ability to ____.

- **a** know when to quit
- **b** keep trying
- **c** avoid challenges

2 **Persistence helps people____.**

- **a** keep focused on goals during difficulties
- **b** figure out ways to move past obstacles
- **c** avoid overwhelming situations

3 **The word *yet* is powerful because you ____.**

- **a** target your effort and practice
- **b** understand you only improve by working harder
- **c** face setbacks with optimism

4 **People with a growth mindset ____.**

- **a** believe intelligence can be developed
- **b** understand some failures show our stopping points
- **c** exist in a world of possibility

5 **Rosa is a restaurant manager. She wants to be an example of the *yet* attitude for her employees. What should she do?**

- **a** Analyze what has not worked well.
- **b** Monitor the results so she can make changes.
- **c** Demonstrate how hard work is the only way to feel successful.

6 **Fatma is an insurance agent. Recently, she has not met her sales goals and is feeling very discouraged. What can she do to stay focused and reach her goals?**

- **a** Reflect on her current strategies to understand what she is doing.
- **b** Realize she can use this chance to change her mindset.
- **c** Realize she is not good at insurance sales and consider changing jobs.

7 **Yan is an engineer. She understands that there will always be things she has not figured out. Which actions show her *yet* attitude?**

- **a** She realizes she is on a learning path.
- **b** She focuses on whether new strategies help her.
- **c** She stays positive but realizes setbacks show her limitations.

8 **Andre started working for a company that takes care of lawns and gardens. He realized there is so much he needs to learn that he is starting to lose interest. What strategies should he use to give him renewed persistence in learning?**

- **a** Get other employees' guidance.
- **b** Ask his supervisor questions.
- **c** Figure things out alone so the company owner is impressed.

Check your understanding 8

REFRESH YOUR MEMORY!
Review the Online Course material in your Resources.

Choose the best answers. More than one answer may be correct in some items.

1 **Good habits of wellness include ____.**
- **a** finding ways to relax
- **b** having good sleeping habits
- **c** prioritizing work in daily routines

2 **When people prioritize wellness, they ____.**
- **a** miss less work because of sickness
- **b** have lower stress levels
- **c** feel there is not enough time for everything

3 **What steps should you take to evaluate your personal routines?**
- **a** Find out how you spend your time.
- **b** Notice how to spend more time on healthy habits.
- **c** Pay attention to how to make challenging changes.

4 **Evaluating and improving personal routines helps you ____.**
- **a** make healthy changes
- **b** feel more motivated
- **c** use your time more efficiently

5 **Ming's company recently sent out an email about the importance of wellness, encouraging employees to evaluate their personal routines. What suggestions would the email make?**
- **a** Think about small changes that you can make.
- **b** Focus on wellness on the weekends when you are less busy.
- **c** Consider only your mental health.

6 **Min-ji has noticed she has less energy than before. She wants to replace some unhealthy habits with healthy ones. Which should she do?**
- **a** Replace her afternoon coffee with herbal tea.
- **b** Take a walk rather than check social media.
- **c** Make big changes to have the best results.

7 **Sue has started to replace some unhealthy habits with healthy ones. What can she do to maintain these good habits?**
- **a** Exercise with a friend.
- **b** Check off days when she achieves her target.
- **c** Watch more TV to reduce stress.

8 **Ayumi has started eating healthier meals, but it takes more time to cook so she is getting tired of trying to keep this habit. What can she do to maintain this healthy habit?**
- **a** Reward herself for meeting goals.
- **b** Share her eating goals with another person.
- **c** On the weekends, take a break from cooking healthy meals.

Check your understanding 9

REFRESH YOUR MEMORY!

Review the Online Course material in your Resources.

Choose the best answers. More than one answer may be correct in some items.

1 **Businesses benefit from giving back because ____.**
- **a** managers can see who has more free time
- **b** it gives them a good reputation
- **c** they are helping those who buy their products

2 **When workers give back through company-led projects, they ____.**
- **a** are offered promotions more quickly
- **b** have team-building experiences
- **c** are able to show different skills

3 **When people who are not currently working give back, they benefit because ____.**
- **a** they gain experience
- **b** they quit wasting time
- **c** they are more attractive to companies

4 **When you are not working for a company, you can give back by ____.**
- **a** considering which causes you want to support
- **b** finding organizations with free meals
- **c** creating a fundraiser or starting an organization

5 **You work for a large, international corporation. You want to organize a volunteer effort to help people after a recent flood. What should you do?**
- **a** Find out about current company programs.
- **b** Ask about company donation matches.
- **c** Realize everyone is too busy to help this time.

6 **You are a manager for a small company that does not have any give back programs. You want to help employees so they volunteer to read to kids at the library. What can you do?**
- **a** Share your ideas with the company owner.
- **b** Organize a program with your co-workers.
- **c** Ask the company for incentives before you start anything.

7 **Max is looking for a job, but since he is not working, he has some extra time. He wants to find ways to get involved and give back. What should he do?**
- **a** Decide which causes he cares about.
- **b** Consider whether he can do the tasks an organization needs help with.
- **c** Find an organization that puts their volunteer lists online so he gets noticed.

8 **Runa noticed the park near her home always has lots of trash and is not taken care of. She looked for an organization that she could volunteer with to clean the park, but she could not find one. What should she do?**
- **a** Consider creating the organization.
- **b** Find another cause to support.
- **c** Start cleaning the park with friends.

Check your understanding 10

REFRESH YOUR MEMORY!
Review the Online Course material in your Resources.

Choose the best answers. More than one answer may be correct in some items.

1 **To build your personal brand online, you should ____.**
- **a** use a nickname in your email
- **b** think about the message your photos convey
- **c** avoid a headshot or profile picture

2 **To protect your private information, you should ____.**
- **a** have a separate, private profile that employers cannot find
- **b** use privacy settings to control who sees the information
- **c** become friends with every co-worker who sends an online request

3 **To build a strong personal brand, you should ____.**
- **a** have a profile on job networking sites if you want a new job
- **b** not include specific skills in your headline and summary
- **c** notice and use key words like people in your industry

4 **How can you use social media to further your career?**
- **a** Make sure your profile is updated and relevant.
- **b** Show pictures of parties and social events with co-workers.
- **c** Stay credible so you get noticed when it is time for promotions.

5 **Ike only has one social media profile. He knows his manager uses the same social media site and can possibly see what he posts. What should he do?**
- **a** Check what information is in his "About Me" section.
- **b** Only have friends see some information.
- **c** Create a professional profile with a username that is not his name.

6 **Anika is a salesperson in a family-owned store. She would like to use this experience to work in sales for a non-profit company. Her online profile includes a lot of information about her experiences and likes. What should she add to develop a strong online brand for potential employers?**
- **a** The names of places where she volunteered.
- **b** The names of organizations she belongs to.
- **c** The names of companies she likes.

7 **Yemi is moving to a new city with his family, and he is looking for a new job as an administrative assistant. He created an online profile on a job networking site, using the username YemiOnTheMove. He posted photos of his family packing up their car to move, and he included a document with links to his favorite gaming websites. How can he improve his profile?**
- **a** Show more pictures of his family.
- **b** Use a more straightforward username.
- **c** Consider the links and the message they give.

8 **Rosa works for an international trading company. On a job networking site, she often talks about how she does not like working every weekend and hopes to move to a new company soon. She is worried about privacy, so she has a headline and summary but not much else on her profile. What should she do to build her brand?**
- **a** Stop complaining about her current company.
- **b** Attach her résumé.
- **c** Add specific key words with her hobbies and the names of companies she likes.

Check your understanding 11

REFRESH YOUR MEMORY!
Review the Online Course material in your Resources.

Choose the best answers. More than one answer may be correct in some items.

1 **To start finding a company that is right for you, you should search job listings online ____.**

- **a** using words that describe the skills you want to have
- **b** using keywords from your résumé
- **c** using words describing your experience

2 **When you gather background information about a company, you look at a company's website to see if a company is a good match for you. You can find information such as ____.**

- **a** their goals and leadership team
- **b** their products or services
- **c** the values of their employees

3 **In the "Jobs/Career" section of a company's website, you can find ____.**

- **a** specifics about a job you heard about at a job fair
- **b** the company's business plan and current projects
- **c** information about all the open jobs in the company

4 **By researching companies, you ____.**

- **a** will have confidence the company is right for you
- **b** can create a longer list of potential companies
- **c** will be able to have a better job interview

5 **Trung likes his job as an assistant manager, but he really likes customer service and leading teams. He feels his company does not focus enough on service and does not give him enough leadership opportunities. He is thinking about changing jobs. To begin researching companies and find out if a company is right for him, he should look at ____.**

- **a** a website comparing salary ranges from different companies
- **b** the Careers section on the company's website
- **c** the company's About Us on their customer website

6 **Gemma is looking for her first full-time job. She has been researching companies and narrowed down her choices. She wants to dig deeper to learn more about two companies' future prospects. How can she get more information?**

- **a** Check with alumni groups for contacts.
- **b** Talk with connections at the companies.
- **c** Read the Jobs and Careers section on their website.

7 **Saif is moving to a new city to be closer to his family. He is an experienced painter and has a reputation for working hard and being very skilled at what he does. He wants to find a job with a company that will be a good fit for him. What should he do?**

- **a** Narrow his choices to companies that will value his experience.
- **b** Search companies that have offices in many different locations.
- **c** Do research on each company's website and social media sites.

8 **Lena is an administrative assistant, but she wants to start selling insurance. She heard about a company that could be a great place for her to work. She has been invited for an interview. She has read About the Company on their website, but now wants to find in-depth information. What should she do next?**

- **a** Prepare a list of questions to get the full inside scoop from her interviewer.
- **b** Talk to people who know the company goals and products.
- **c** Read the Market Specific Solutions section on the company website.

Check your understanding 12

REFRESH YOUR MEMORY!
Review the Online Course material in your Resources.

Choose the best answers. More than one answer may be correct in some items.

1 You should ____ during an interview.
  a be positive
  b demonstrate your forward-thinking attitude
  c avoid explaining large gaps between jobs

2 During an interview, when asked about a skill you do not have, it is important to ____.
  a discuss what you are able to do
  b say you are willing to learn
  c avoid looking too eager to get the job

3 You should get ready for an interview by ____.
  a considering what the interviewer wants to know
  b changing your résumé as necessary
  c practicing answers to questions often asked in interviews

4 During an interview, when there are difficult questions about skills you need for the job but do not have, what should you say?
  a "I don't have the skills you're looking for in a candidate."
  b "I'm an eager learner and can work on my weaknesses."
  c "I learned a lot in my previous job and can use that with you and your company."

5 Dan fixes air conditioning systems. He often disagreed with the manager in his previous company, and he was fired. He should ____ when he is asked about his previous job.
  a emphasize how difficult it was to work with the manager
  b give a brief explanation of what happened and then move on
  c say that he made the decision to leave

6 Fatma got an email asking her to have an interview for a job at a company she really wants to work at. To get ready for the interview, she should ____.
  a practice exactly what she wants to say
  b make up some answers to look stronger
  c brainstorm questions she may be asked

7. Trung is interviewing for his first job as a teacher. He was asked a question he does not know how to respond to. In this situation, it is important to ____.
  a remain calm
  b think out loud
  c avoid asking for time to think

8 Sonia wants to start working as a store manager. During her job interview at the new company, she is asked what she would do to increase sales of a specific product. She had not prepared to answer this question. She should ____.
  a talk about everything she knows about the product
  b say she did not prepare for the question so she cannot answer
  c talk about the types of customers she imagines will use the product

DISCUSSION STRATEGIES

Discussion strategies

When you are in class or at work, you may need to take part in discussions. To successfully participate, you can use a number of different kinds of strategies. They include strategies that help you:

1. Work with others
2. Clarify what you hear or clarify what you say
3. Get and stay involved in the discussion
4. Organize your ideas

During each discussion in class, choose one kind of strategy you want to improve or one you think will be useful. Pick a phrase and try to use it during the in-class activities. Remember to always say the phrase in a polite way.

You can listen to the phrases and examples ▶.

1 Working with others

Some strategies can make it easier to work with other people who are part of the discussion. If you can, try starting the discussion or helping to keep the discussion moving in the right direction. These strategies can help.

Management strategies	Sample phrases
a Starting the discussion	▶ Is everyone ready? ▶ Let's get started. ▶ Who wants to start?
b Asking others to participate	▶ Who wants to answer? ▶ Does anyone have anything to add? ▶ Who wants to jump in?
c Helping specific people to get involved	▶ Alex, what do you think? ▶ Do you have anything to add, Lu? ▶ Minnie, any thoughts on this?
d Jumping in with talkative people	▶ That's a good idea, and it would be great to hear from everyone else. ▶ OK, thanks! And what does everyone else think? ▶ Great point, Marco! Now, why don't we see what some others think?
e Staying on the topic	▶ That's interesting, but maybe I'm missing something. I don't see how that's really relevant. ▶ Let's discuss this later. For now, we need to stay on task. ▶ Sorry, but I don't think that's really related to our topic.
f Keeping the discussion moving	▶ OK. So now let's move on to the next issue. ▶ That's a good point. We can talk about that next time. ▶ I'm afraid that we're going to run out of time if we don't move on.
g Telling someone you can't hear them*	▶ I'm sorry. I didn't hear what you said. ▶ Can you speak a little louder, please? ▶ Sorry! What was that?
h Telling someone they speak too fast*	▶ I'm sorry. Can you say that a little slower? ▶ Can you speak more slowly, please? ▶ Sorry. I didn't catch that.

*You can also use clarification strategies to make sure you understood someone who is quiet or talks too quickly.

Discussion strategies

2 Clarifying

Sometimes it is hard for you to understand what someone is saying or for others to understand you. Clarifying is a natural part of discussions. Even native speakers use these strategies because not everyone understands everything all the time!

Clarification strategies	Sample phrases	Examples
a Clarifying (when you didn't understand someone else)	▶ Sorry, but I don't understand. ▶ I'm not sure what you mean by that. ▶ I didn't follow what you said. ▶ I'm not sure what you're getting at.	
b Restating (when someone doesn't understand you)	In other words . . . By that, I mean . . .	▶ **A:** You're more likely to be remembered if you have a strong brand. **B:** Sorry, but I don't really understand. **A:** In other words, a strong personal brand will help people remember you. ▶ **A:** Identify your transferable skills and consider how to develop them. **B:** I'm not sure what you mean by transferable. **A:** By that, I mean skills that are useful in different situations and different jobs.
c Checking (when you want to make sure someone understands you)	▶ Just checking—do you know what I mean? ▶ Is that clear? Does anyone have any questions? ▶ Does that make sense?	
d Paraphrasing (what the speaker says)	Are you saying that . . . Do you mean that . . .	▶ **A:** Miscommunication can lead to a lot of expensive mistakes. **B:** Are you saying that the company could lose profits if we don't communicate well? ▶ **A:** I think this is going to be hard. We're going to have some resistance. **B:** Do you mean that they're going to push back on that idea?
e Paraphrasing (what someone else says)	Alan said that . . . What . . . means is . . .	▶ Alan said that it's important to build rapport with both colleagues and clients. ▶ What Fara means is that creating an environment of respect is the best way to prevent conflict.

Discussion strategies

3 Getting involved

It can be challenging to participate in discussions. Sometimes you have to involve yourself without being asked, keep your turn (if others try to interrupt you), interrupt (when others are talking), and get your turn back (after being interrupted).

Participation strategies	Sample phrases	Examples
a Getting involved	▶ Can I ask a question? ▶ I have something I'd like to say. ▶ I can offer some input on this topic.	
b Keeping your turn	▶ Excuse me, but I'd just like to finish what I'm saying. ▶ Sorry, but could you give me one more second to finish? ▶ It won't take me long to say this.	
c Interrupting	Excuse me . . . Sorry to interrupt . . . Can I add to . . .	▶ Excuse me, but I'd like to add something. ▶ Sorry to interrupt, but I have a question. ▶ Can I add to what you just said?
d Getting your turn back	As I was saying . . . Going back to what I was saying . . . In any case . . .	▶ As I was saying, good leaders are ones who make tough decisions. ▶ Going back to what I was saying, team members really appreciate motivational leaders. ▶ In any case, people appreciate good leaders even if they don't always agree with their decisions.
e Commenting (on what someone has said)	That's a good point . . . I see what you mean . . . I'm afraid I have to disagree . . .	▶ That's a good point, Misato. ▶ I see what you mean, Kelly. ▶ I'm afraid I have to disagree with you, Jun.
f Adding (to what someone has said)	I agree with you . . . and also . . . Another thing to consider is . . . I have something to add to that.	▶ I agree with you about making money, Margaret, and also, we need to make sure the customers are happy. ▶ Yes, and another thing to consider is the best way to communicate respectfully. ▶ What Mei said is true, and I have something to add to that.

Discussion strategies

4 Organizing

Lastly, organization techniques can help communication and make discussion easier to follow.

Organization techniques	Sample words and phrases	Examples
a Chronological	First . . . second . . . third . . . Next . . . then . . . later	▶ First, let's talk about active listening. Second, we'll discuss how to speak respectfully. Third, we'll make a plan to prevent conflict. ▶ Next, we'll talk about setting a schedule. Then, we'll talk about including deadlines. Later, we'll discuss how we need to be open to changes.
b Cause and effect	If . . . , then . . . When . . ., then . . .	▶ If you admit your mistakes, then you're more likely to earn the respect of the person who is upset. ▶ When you listen actively, then you're more likely to understand why someone is upset.
c Categorical	There are five ways . . . The main things . . .	▶ There are five ways to manage conflict. ▶ The main thing to do is to communicate respectfully.
d Problem and solution	The main problem is . . . One big issue is . . . The best solution is . . . We could . . .	▶ The main problem is that we aren't managing our time well. ▶ One big issue is we don't have regular staff meetings. ▶ The best solution is the one that makes the customers happy and makes the company money. ▶ We could brainstorm ideas and then discuss which one is best.
e Adding an idea	On top of that . . . In the same way . . .	▶ Personal branding is a good way to advance your career. On top of that, it helps people remember you. ▶ Networking is a good way to meet people who are working in your field. In the same way, conferences can also be a good way to find others who have the same type of job you want.
f Contrast	Although . . . However . . .	▶ Although teamwork is an important skill, independence is equally valuable to employers. ▶ We read and hear information from a lot of different sources every day. However, not all of these sources will be reliable.

VOCABULARY PRACTICE

Vocabulary practice 1

Exercise (A)

Complete the puzzle.

Across

1 to make something clearer by giving more information about it
4 to increase the range of things you know about or experience
6 to remember information
8 to attract and hold the attention of someone
9 to concentrate on one particular thing
10 paying close attention

Down

2 to bring something back to your mind
3 easily annoyed by others' mistakes or because you have to wait
5 expressions or movements used as a signal instead of words
7 to do multiple things at one time

Exercise (B)

Use the correct words from the puzzle to complete the notes.

HOW TO BE AN ACTIVE LISTENER IN THE WORKPLACE

- *Keep eye contact with the speaker and listen carefully. Show the speaker that you're* [1] ____________ *.* *Don't do other things when you are listening. If you* [2] ____________ *, you won't be able to pay full attention.*
- *Try to* [3] ____________ *on the speaker's body language as well as what they're saying. Sometimes* [4] ____________ *show a person's feelings better than their words.*
- *Taking notes while listening to the speaker can help you* [5] ____________ *the information. A good way to take notes is to record the speaker so you can stay focused during the speech.*
- *Try not to get* [6] ____________ *if there's something you don't understand during the speech because you can ask the speaker to* [7] ____________ *at the end or reach out to them later.*

Vocabulary practice 2

Exercise (A)

Read the clues and find the words.

I	S	M	A	T	Y	S	S	O	I	O	P	E	N
N	H	A	T	E	A	S	E	F	L	C	G	P	K
A	B	K	M	C	U	S	T	O	M	E	R	C	A
P	G	F	O	U	N	D	A	T	I	O	N	O	T
P	H	I	S	G	E	S	T	U	R	E	Z	M	T
R	S	C	P	M	C	F	I	G	C	E	B	M	E
O	H	E	H	A	I	S	P	T	H	S	Y	O	N
P	U	B	E	T	N	V	H	J	E	T	C	N	T
R	T	R	R	K	T	J	S	N	C	A	E	G	I
I	D	E	E	B	E	R	P	Q	K	B	B	R	V
A	O	A	J	D	R	P	S	D	I	L	X	O	E
T	W	K	B	H	A	R	M	O	N	I	O	U	S
E	N	E	H	W	C	L	E	M	C	S	Y	N	L
S	F	R	M	U	T	U	A	L	I	H	G	D	F

1 I felt very angry when he made a(n) ___________ comment about my appearance.
2 If you ___________ people ___________ when they disagree, they won't approach you again with their ideas.
3 It is my responsibility as the manager to help everyone on my team feel ___________.
4 It's important to build a solid ___________ of trust among the team members.
5 There is quite a friendly ___________ at Sarah's workplace.
6 Customers always like Jason because he is very friendly when they ___________ with him.
7 Success in our business depends on ___________ relationships with customers.
8 My manager and I have a lot of ___________ respect for each other.
9 Chris is ___________ to suggestions, so don't hesitate to talk to him about your idea.
10 If we want to resolve this conflict, we need to find ___________.
11 Sarah wants to ___________ good relationships with her co-workers so that they can work together effectively.
12 I was happy that the audience listening to my presentation was ___________.

Exercise (B)

Use the correct words from the puzzle to complete the conversations.

1

I have been working so hard to create a happy 1 ___________ in the office.

I know. Your positive attitude makes everyone feel 2 ___________.

2

I think Gary is really respectful. He avoids 3 ___________ topics when talking with co-workers.

Yes, he puts great value in establishing 4 ___________ relationships with everyone.

3

Is the new manager 5 ___________ to new ideas coming from the employees?

Yes, I've heard that she doesn't 6 ___________ people ___________ when they share different opinions with her.

Vocabulary practice 3

Exercise A

Complete the puzzle. What is the vertical word?

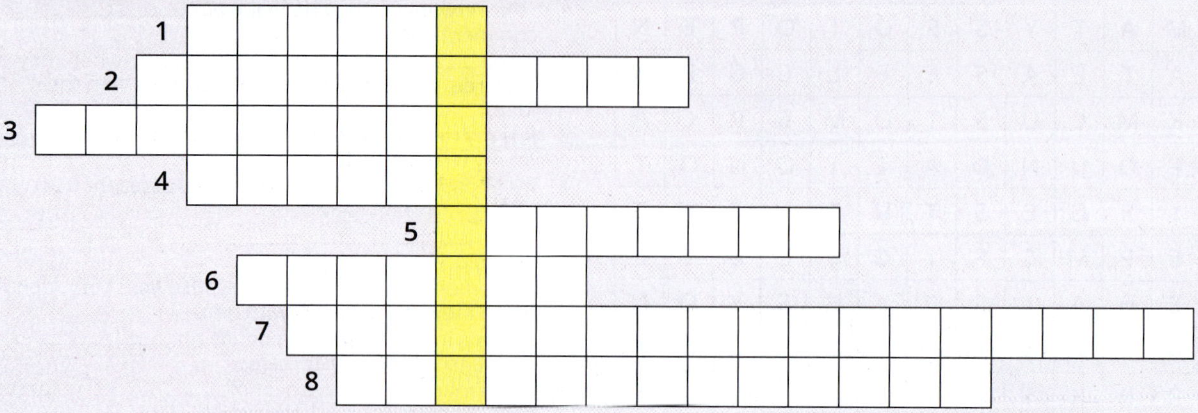

1 to make small changes to make something better or more effective: *to* ______________ *your career plans*
2 done in a planned way: *a(n)* ______________ *move*
3 relating to a short period of time: *a(n)* ______________ *goal*
4 to try to achieve a goal over a long period of time: *to* ______________ *a career in finance*
5 relating to a long period of time: *a(n)* ______________ *strategy*
6 to change the way in which something is organized: *to* ______________ *your goals*
7 existing abilities that can be used in a new situation: ______________ *are critical when changing fields*
8 an event or experience that helps you progress towards another thing: *take this job as a(n)* ______________

Exercise B

Use the correct words from the puzzle to complete an employee's journal.

How to set realistic career goals

- *Identify my interests. Decide on a field in which I want to* [1] ______________ *a career.*
- *Set a* [2] ______________ *goal; a goal I can see myself achieving in five years or more. Then break it down into* [3] ______________ *goals; goals I can achieve in a year or less.*
- *Create a career path* [4] ______________ *that shows where I will start and end. Treat each stage of my career as a* [5] ______________ *that will lead to the next one.*
- *Look for* [6] ______________ *that I have learned in my current job. Think about how I can use them to apply for my next one.*
- *Evaluate my progress frequently.* [7] ______________ *my plans along the way if necessary.*

Vocabulary practice 4

Exercise A

Complete the puzzle.

Across

3 to reach an agreement where each party gives up something
6 to say that a person is responsible for something going wrong
8 to become greater or more serious
10 the level of confidence and positive feelings that a group of people have
11 expressing negative judgement
12 to help develop and improve over a period of time

Down

1 to express that a person did something good or important
2 quick to protect oneself from criticism
4 the act of stopping something from happening
5 a wide range of different people, things, or ideas
7 to quickly come up with a lot of ideas
9 including a wide range of people or things

Exercise B

Use the correct words from the puzzle to complete the conversations.

1

I think the 1 ____________ of my team helps us create great projects. When different people contribute to any ideas, the results are better.

You're very lucky to be working in a(n) 2 ____________ workplace where everyone is welcome.

2

If you want to 3 ____________ good relationships with your co-workers, you should focus on the good work they have done.

You're right, but sometimes I can't stop myself from being 4 ____________ of their mistakes. I need to learn how to give constructive feedback.

3

Let's 5 ____________ some ideas together and come up with a list of suggestions.

I agree. This way, we can work more quickly. It can also help to build 6 ____________ in the office.

4

If managers constantly 7 ____________ their employees for mistakes and not take any responsibility themselves, they lose their employees' trust.

Yes, it makes employees 8 ____________ and afraid to accept any responsibility.

Vocabulary practice 5

Exercise (A)

Read the clues and find the words.

E	V	R	H	F	L	Y	R	U	I	A	D	V	S
V	A	E	O	E	V	I	D	E	N	C	E	X	O
A	B	L	K	I	D	C	P	S	M	N	T	F	G
L	S	I	R	S	X	R	O	J	V	C	E	S	L
U	O	A	I	C	L	A	I	M	S	I	R	T	C
A	L	B	F	N	Y	G	T	Q	W	T	M	A	R
T	U	L	H	W	F	L	A	W	H	E	I	T	E
E	T	E	B	Y	O	C	J	K	B	J	N	I	D
G	E	M	E	A	S	U	R	A	B	L	E	S	I
V	R	V	P	L	O	G	I	C	A	L	F	T	B
A	C	R	O	S	S	C	H	E	C	K	K	I	L
G	D	U	B	I	A	S	C	R	S	I	M	C	E
U	H	I	W	O	U	T	C	O	M	E	S	S	V
E	C	V	E	R	I	F	Y	R	F	D	U	N	D

1 Before writing the report, try to ____________ if the sources are good or not.

2 I trust this website and its editor, so I believe the information published here is ____________.

3 Aisha supported her argument with enough ____________ from several reports.

4 It's important to ____________ your sources if you want the readers to take your findings seriously.

5 The ____________ show that most employees are more productive working from home.

6 This report isn't ____________. Nobody has heard of the author.

7 She needs to support all her ____________ about the product if she wants to sell it.

8 The team is working hard to fix a(n) ____________ that has recently been found in the product.

9 You shouldn't change your job or career without having ____________ reasons.

10 Reporters shouldn't show any ____________ towards a certain political party.

11 We need an expert in the field to ____________ these numbers in the report.

12 If the rules are ____________, people may interpret them in different ways.

Exercise (B)

Use the correct words from the puzzle to complete a student's notes.

How to check if the information is accurate

To [1] ____________ *that the information I found is accurate, I need to …*

- *check that the statements are not* [2] ____________ *or incomplete.*
- *make sure the numbers add up if any* [3] ____________ *are involved.*
- *see if I can find evidence that supports the* [4] ____________.
- *confirm that the evidence I found comes from a* [5] ____________ *source.*
- *check the background of anyone whose name I want to* [6] ____________.
- *determine whether the evidence supports the statements and if there is any* [7] ____________ *in the logic.*
- *make sure that the statements don't use emotion that show* [8] ____________.

Vocabulary practice 6

Exercise A

Complete the puzzle. What is the vertical word?

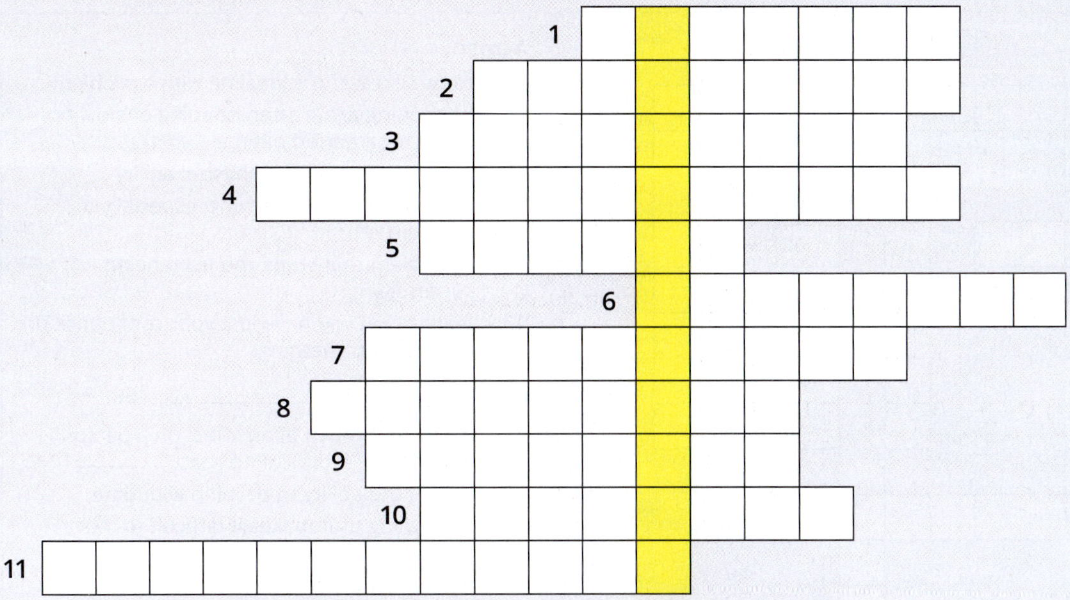

1 to give others the strength and the freedom to do something: *to* ________ *people to make decisions*
2 refusing to accept something: *to be* ________ *to new ideas*
3 achieving the results you want: *to be* ________ *at your job*
4 the activity of working with others: *to work in close* ________ *with the team*
5 an idea of how something should develop: *to have a clear* ________
6 to give a person a reason to do something: *to* ________ *us to achieve the goal*
7 the act of giving others a good reason to do something: *she needed a little* ________
8 to question if something is right or fair: *to* ________ *old beliefs and ideas*
9 a negative reaction: *to give him* ________ *on his ideas*
10 to give someone a duty or job: *to* ________ *a task*
11 aiming to help improve: *to give* ________ *feedback*

Exercise B

Use the correct words from the puzzle to complete the conversations.

1

Prisha is a great supervisor. She knows how to 1 ________ her employees by helping them build confidence to set big goals.

I agree. As a team leader, she is also able to 2 ________ tasks to the right people.

2

Do you think I'm 3 ________ to new ideas as the director?

Well, sometimes you give people 4 ________ on their ideas, but that doesn't mean you aren't open to changes.

3

We were successful in this project because we encouraged 5 ________ and created a great working atmosphere.

Yes, that definitely helped to 6 ________ people to do their best.

Vocabulary practice 7

Exercise A

Complete the puzzle.

Across

3 to be successful in dealing with a problem
6 happening again after stopping or slowing down for a period of time
8 a person's mental or physical ability
10 to come across something, especially a problem
11 a problem that stops you from being successful
12 feeling that you have lost your confidence or interest in something

Down

1 having too much of an effect on a person and making it difficult to react
2 having the ability to develop with time
4 something that makes it difficult to move forward
5 the quality of believing good things will happen
7 ideas or advice that helps a person succeed
9 to make a mistake when you are trying to achieve a goal

Exercise B

Use the correct words from the puzzle to complete the notes.

WAYS TO BE PERSISTENT

- Set a goal and make a plan. Think about the skills you have, and believe that you have the 1 ______________ to achieve your goals.
- Don't give up when you are faced with a(n) 2 ______________. Keep a positive attitude because 3 ______________ can help you deal with difficulty.
- If you feel 4 ______________ by challenges, get motivated by the thought of success.
- Remember that it's common to 5 ______________ now and then on your way to success. What's important is to get back up and 6 ______________ the problems.
- If everything gets too 7 ______________ and stressful, imagine yourself achieving your goal. This will give you 8 ______________ energy to get back to work when you feel down.

Vocabulary practice 8

Exercise (A)

Read the clues and find the words.

A	S	E	M	E	D	I	T	A	T	E	V	F	N
C	A	X	O	L	K	W	U	F	G	I	C	P	U
C	D	I	E	T	O	D	R	A	I	N	A	R	T
O	N	H	P	M	E	I	X	P	H	M	L	O	R
U	M	A	T	H	L	E	T	I	C	U	S	V	I
N	A	A	V	L	N	U	C	Y	D	M	T	E	T
T	X	P	R	I	O	R	I	T	Y	O	G	N	I
A	O	S	T	A	R	E	A	T	S	T	H	B	O
B	U	A	I	M	P	F	J	S	O	I	A	Z	U
L	T	X	R	E	P	L	A	C	E	V	B	V	S
E	C	U	L	I	N	A	R	Y	R	E	I	N	W
S	W	E	E	T	T	O	O	T	H	T	T	U	S
F	O	R	M	U	L	A	Z	A	C	B	S	V	E
G	E	B	E	N	C	O	M	P	A	S	S	E	S

1 If anything goes wrong with the project, they will hold the supervisor ______________.

2 A(n) ______________ that includes fruits and vegetables will help you stay healthy.

3 She has a few ______________ that help keep her fit, including going for a walk every morning.

4 Marty is very ______________; he loves to play all kinds of sports.

5 A person's well-being ______________ both physical health and mental health.

6 Spending too much time on the screen will ______________ your energy.

7 If you ______________ soda with water, you will feel better.

8 My parents ______________ every morning to start the day with a clear mind.

9 Their healthy lifestyle is based on a simple ______________; eat a variety of food and be active.

10 Mental health should be considered a ______________ in a highly competitive world.

11 It is a ______________ fact that getting enough sleep improves your productivity during the day.

12 Young people need to eat ______________ meals to fuel not only their bodies, but also their brains.

Exercise (B)

Use the correct words from the puzzle to complete the conversations.

1

I'm trying to develop some healthy 1 ______________. Would you like to play tennis with me on Saturdays?

I'd love to but, honestly, I'm not very 2 ______________; I'm not interested in sports.

2

You look so happy and energetic! What is your 3 ______________ for being so healthy?

It's actually pretty simple! I've made some changes to my diet and decided to 4 ______________ all the chocolate I eat with fruit.

3

My lack of sleep lately is starting to 5 ______________ my energy.

Try to 6 ______________ before going to bed. That might help.

Vocabulary practice 9

Exercise A

Complete the puzzle. What is the vertical word?

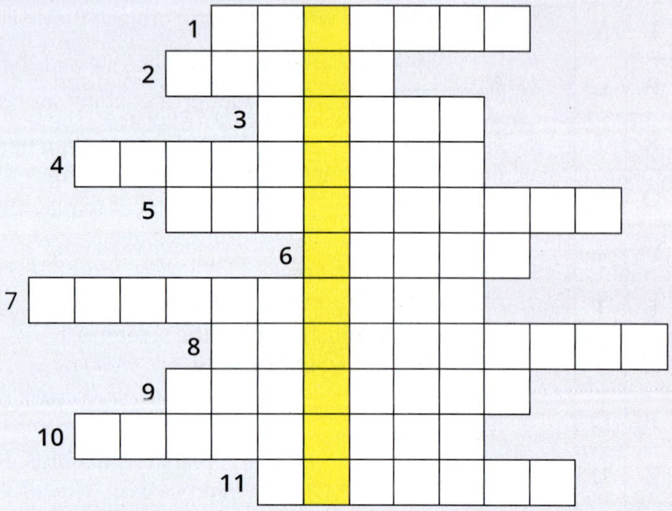

1 having the ability to do something: *to be* ____________ *of managing the team*
2 relating to the standards of good or bad behavior: ____________ *values*
3 an effort and strong desire to achieve something: *to have the* ____________ *to achieve a goal*
4 something that motivates a person: *to provide a(n)* ____________ *to work harder*
5 a legal or moral duty that you must do: *to have a(n)* ____________ *to tell the truth*
6 a belief or organization that people fight for: *an important* ____________
7 an event planned to raise money for a specific purpose, especially to help someone: *to organize a(n)* ____________
8 overall quality or character judged by people in general: *to have a good/bad* ____________
9 money given to help a person or an organization: *to give a(n)* ____________
10 to offer to do something without expecting anything in return: *to* ____________ *to help*
11 to build relationships with people for employment or business: *to* ____________ *with people*

Exercise B

Use the correct words from the puzzle to complete an employee's notes from a seminar about social responsibility in business.

Advantages of Giving Back

For companies:

- *Meeting their moral* [1] ____________ *as a company by doing the right thing.*
- *Building a positive* [2] ____________ *to attract more customers and better employees.*
- *Creating a good working atmosphere so employees have the* [3] ____________ *to work harder.*
- *Receiving money from the government as a(n)* [4] ____________ *for helping the community.*

For employees:

- *Showing what you are* [5] ____________ *of outside of work.*
- *Finding an opportunity to meet and* [6] ____________ *with new people.*
- *Feeling a greater sense of satisfaction by working for a good* [7] ____________.

Vocabulary practice 10

Exercise (A)

Complete the puzzle.

Across

4 the belief that work is a valuable activity
5 connected with what is happening or being said
6 can be seen or noticed
7 a belief or opinion based on how things seem
9 part of someone's character that affects their mood and behavior
10 careful in choosing
11 the fact or state of being in a place

Down

1 always happening or behaving in a similar way
2 the part of a website that allows you to control who sees your information
3 to show or describe a person or a thing
8 real, honest, or sincere

Exercise (B)

Use the correct words from the puzzle to complete the conversations.

1

It's important to be 1 ____________ about the photos you share online. Some employers look up candidates' activity on social media before hiring.

Yes, that's why I have changed my 2 ____________ so that only my close friends can see my online activity.

2

Dave has such a strong 3 ____________ at work, his personality really lifts everyone.

Yes, he is also very hardworking because of his 4 ____________.

3

I think that, as a company, we need to work more on the image that we want to 5 ____________ online.

I agree, but the image has to be 6 ____________. We can't pretend to be something that we're not.

4

What is your 7 ____________ of the new CEO?

Well, she has a lovely 8 ____________. She is calm and very kind to everyone.

Vocabulary practice 11

Exercise (A)

Complete the puzzle. What is the vertical word?

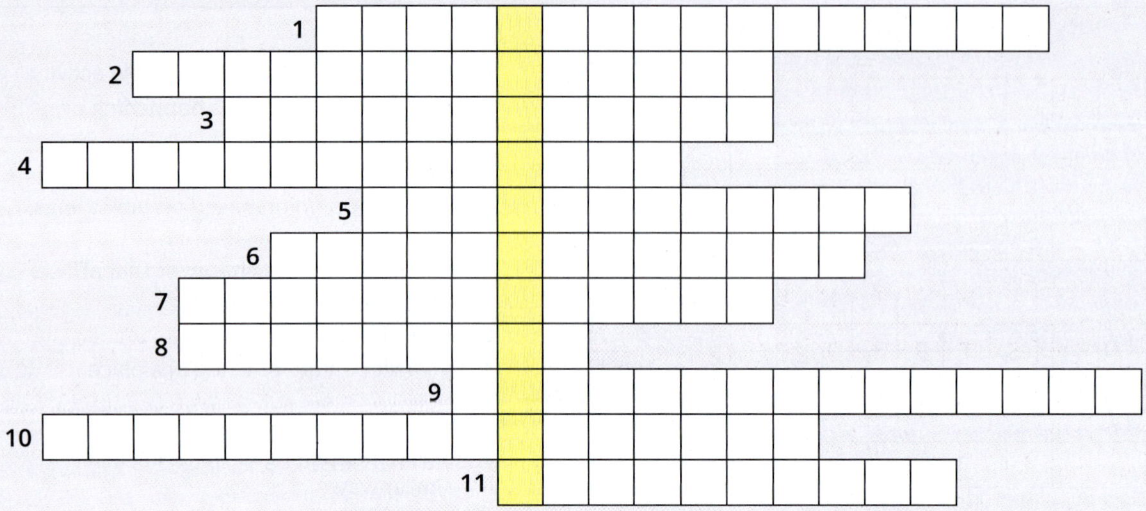

1 a short description of the purpose of a company or organization: *read the company's* ____________

2 research done to learn more about something: *to do* ____________ *about a company*

3 a document that describes a company's goal and its plan to achieve it: *to submit a* ____________

4 to limit the number of competing options: *to* ____________ *of possibilities*

5 careful and detailed examination of a business deal before agreeing to it: *to exercise* ____________

6 all the information about a field of interest: *to have a large* ____________

7 the act of entering certain words on the internet to find out more about something: *to do a(n)* ____________

8 in a short form that is easy to see or understand with a quick look: *to see* ____________

9 the amount of time you spend at your job compared with the amount of time you spend with your family or doing what you enjoy: *to have a good* ____________

10 the possibility of being successful in the distant future: *good* ____________

11 the quality of being completely suitable for something: *to be a* ____________ *for a position*

Exercise (B)

Use the correct words from the puzzle to complete a student's notes from a workshop.

How to Find the Perfect Position for You

- Consider my qualifications and [1] ____________ .
- Do a [2] ____________ to find job listings relevant to my skills.
- Try to [3] ____________ of my options by eliminating the ones that don't excite me.
- Do some [4] ____________ on the company if a position attracts me.
- Read the [5] ____________ of the company to see if I agree with their values.
- Look for the company's [6] ____________ on their website to learn about their future projects.
- Know that it might not be possible to find the [7] ____________ for me.

Vocabulary practice 12

Exercise A

Read the clues and find the words.

T	F	E	L	P	B	A	O	I	Z	S	U	D	J
A	O	A	D	O	P	P	B	U	Y	T	I	M	E
K	L	G	K	T	R	P	T	J	N	U	Y	K	N
E	L	E	O	E	E	L	M	D	K	M	I	H	P
T	O	R	V	N	S	Y	P	L	B	P	F	U	E
H	W	T	E	T	E	L	M	A	C	H	E	T	E
E	U	O	R	I	N	S	T	R	A	T	E	G	Y
L	P	T	C	A	T	O	M	J	Y	I	F	N	C
E	J	E	O	L	H	G	A	P	Y	E	A	R	T
A	T	A	M	B	S	E	L	F	D	O	U	B	T
D	I	M	E	M	P	H	A	S	I	Z	E	L	B
P	D	L	H	S	T	R	A	N	D	E	D	Y	Z
O	N	T	H	E	S	P	O	T	B	M	T	K	U
K	C	L	A	R	I	F	I	C	A	T	I	O	N

1 Clive should __________ on this project because he is the most experienced in this area.

2 The company's __________ to increase sales has been effective.

3 During a job interview, you should __________ your strengths relevant to the position.

4 It's a good idea to prepare for challenging questions that might __________ you at an interview.

5 There are steps you can follow to connect with __________ customers.

6 When you feel any __________, try to remind yourself of your qualifications and skills.

7 It is sometimes important to ask for help if you want to __________ a problem you have.

8 I can't give you all the details __________ without referring to my notes.

9 It will leave a good impression if you __________ with an email after an interview.

10 Dressing formally to a meeting helps you __________ yourself as a professional.

11 Marie was asked a lot of questions for __________ because her presentation wasn't clear enough.

12 We need to __________ so we can review the figures again before agreeing to the deal.

Exercise B

Use the correct words from the puzzle to complete the conversations.

1

What do I need to do to 1 __________ myself as a confident and reliable team leader?

I think the first step is to remind yourself of your achievements and free yourself from 2 __________.

2

How can we 3 __________ these challenges we've had in sales?

Improving our customer service is a(n) 4 __________ we can adopt.

3

I really want to 5 __________ on this project. I think I'm ready for the responsibility.

Then, you should 6 __________ your contributions to the projects so far in the meeting tomorrow.

4

I'm really worried about the interview tomorrow. What if they ask questions that just 7 __________ me?

I heard that a good way to deal with that is to 8 __________ by asking for clarification so you can think about your answer.

Glossary

Module 1: Communication 1

doable* (adj) able to be completed or done
eye-catching* (adj) something eye-catching is unusual or attractive in a way that makes you notice it
flashy* (adj) too big, bright, or expensive in a way that other people disapprove of
get on sth* (phr) start doing sth
souvenir (n) an object that you keep to remind yourself of a special occasion or place you have visited

Module 2: Communication 2

accomplishment (n) something successful or impressive that is achieved after a lot of effort and hard work
check in with (phr v) contact someone to confirm that there are no problems
gesture (n) a movement of your arms, hands or head that shows what you mean or how you feel
icebreaker (n) something that you say or do to make people less nervous when they first meet

Module 3: Goal Setting

firsthand (adj) experience, knowledge, an account, etc. that has been learned or gained by doing something yourself
hostess (n) a woman who takes people to their table in a restaurant
learning difficulty (phr) a condition that makes it difficult for someone to learn as quickly or in the same way as most other people
metaphor (n) a way of describing something by comparing it to something else that has similar qualities, without using the word "like" or "as"
pursue* (v) to continue doing an activity or trying to achieve something over a long period of time
reservation (n) an arrangement made so that a place is kept for you in a hotel, restaurant, airplane, etc.
special (n) a particular product that is sold for a lower price at a particular time

Module 4: Teamwork

bring sth to the table (phr v) contribute to the discussion
individually (adv) separately
jot down (phr v) write a short piece of information quickly

Module 5: Critical Thinking

dreamy (adj) beautiful, very pleasant
ethical (adj) morally correct
gravely ill (phr) very sick
SUV (phr) Sports Utility Vehicle; a large car that can travel on rough ground
texture (n) the way something feels when you touch it

***** in audio

Module 6: Leadership

integrate (v) to join in the life and customs of a group or society, or to help someone do this
software (n) the programs that tell a computer how to do a particular job
understaffed (adj) when a company does not have enough employees

Module 7: Self-Management

barely* (adv) almost not
devastated (adj) extremely shocked or sad
disloyal (adj) doing or saying things that do not support someone that you have a relationship with
mediocre (adj) not very good
patent (n) the right to make or sell a new invention or product that no one else is allowed to copy for a set period of time, or the official document which gives you this right
prestigious (adj) admired as one of the best and most important
stand in someone's way* (phr) to prevent somebody from doing something

Module 8: Wellness

burden (n) a situation or task that you are responsible for, which is very difficult or worrying
embrace (v) to eagerly accept new ideas, opinions, religions, etc.
hammock (n) a large piece of material or a net that you can sleep on, that hangs between two trees or poles
leftovers (n) food that has not been eaten at the end of a meal, and that was not on anyone's plate
notion (n) an idea, belief, or opinion about something, especially one that you think is wrong
stare at* (phr v) to look at someone or something for a long time without moving your eyes
sweet tooth (phr) liking things that taste like sugar

Module 9: Social Responsibility

culinary arts* (plural noun) a field of study related to preparing, cooking, and serving food
max out* (phr v) to use something such as money or energy or time so that there is none left
motive* (n) the reason why someone does something
non-perishable (adj) food that does not need to go in the refrigerator, e.g. canned food or cereal

Module 10: Branding

controversial (adj) causing a lot of disagreement, because many people have strong opinions about the subject being discussed
get around (phr v) deal successfully with a problem
put off (phr v) to be made to dislike something or not want to do something

Glossary

Module 11: Job Search

alumnus* (pl. alumni) (n) a former student of a school, college, or university

be ahead of the game* (phr v) in a position where you are in control of something, and more successful than your competitors

client base* (n) the clients that form the main part of a company's business

consulting (n) the service of providing information, advice, and training to companies

criterion* (pl. criteria) (n) a fact or standard that you use to judge something or make a decision about something

* in audio

dig around* (phr v) find more information about someone or something

testimonial* (n) a formal written statement describing someone's character and abilities

Module 12: Interviewing

gap year (n) a period of time, usually an academic year, taken by a student as a break between school and university or college education

stranded (adj) a stranded person, animal, or vehicle is in a bad situation that cannot be left without help

Notes